Corporate Fall Guy"

Or

The Ups and Downs of a

TV Anchor/Skydiver

by Arch Deal

With thanks to my friend in the sky, Richard Bach, who gave
me the desire to write but did not give me his talent.

Dedicated to:
Karen, Shari, Doug, Diane and Michelle by a proud father!

3 1969 02131 4272

Library of Congress

Deal, Arch
ISBN: : 978-0-578-08646-0

Printed in the United States of America

Table of Contents

photo by **Tony Hathaway**

In Corporate America, the so-called "fall guy" is the person who always gets the blame if something goes wrong!

In my case, however, it was to the contrary.

I was honored for 10 years to be the "fall guy" for Miller Brewing Company.

And, believe me, it was one of the highest honors bestowed upon me.

The Corporate Fall Guy was the Miller Lite All Star/Miller Celebrity who made hundreds of the grandest entries into football fields, baseball diamonds, NASCAR and Indy racetracks....

Skydiving in,

under a beautiful Miller-logo canopy.

This is my story

My city, Tampa ... where I was a local TV anchor for 20 years.

Me and a few friends doing a "weed-wacker."

Chapter 1
My Story

Doing a narration in Turkey

Perhaps some may consider me the luckiest man alive! Obviously not lucky in love, you'll learn, but lucky in so many other ways! Can you believe, for instance, surviving a fall from three thousand feet…when both of my parachutes failed? I was later named a Miller Lite All Star: one of 35 of the greatest athletes in the nation along with NFL stars, baseball greats, NBA basketball stars, soccer and hockey greats, and a famed author to be bestowed with such a distinction.

I was the corporate "fall guy"…the only skydiver named to join this gathering of greats…among them four-time world surfing champion Corky Carroll and the man who held the long-jump record for almost 20 years, Bob Beamon. For me, gravity did all the work! Step out of an airplane and gravity takes over…plunging you earthward at some 120 miles per hour while you trust a large piece of nylon to slow your descent and land you safely (usually) on your designated target.

To be associated with all these super athletes and personalities was one of the greatest honors I could have dreamed of achieving. It even surpassed a career as a TV anchor that gave me the opportunity to interview everyone from presidents to rock stars. In fact, anyone who made the news was available to face the camera and answer questions.

Not to belittle the newsgathering profession, those were wonderful days even though times have changed dramatically for the media over the years! Reporting the news put me in a position of telling the facts, not opinions. I always felt opinions were for editorials! Telling the stories without sensationalism was always the desire of any dedicated news reporter. Somehow, this has changed! As a reporter I was a registered Independent… and remain one. This way, no one could call me a "darn democrat" or "darn republican." I am neither. I am a conservative!

Communicators and editorialists give you their personal opinions. It should always be accepted as such when it is so labeled. Talk radio hosts will tell you that they are not reporters, they are entertainers. You have the right to turn them off anytime.

Don't believe what your eyes are telling you. All they (the current news media) show are cramped by limitation. "Look with your understanding, what you already know, and you'll see the way to fly," is one of my favorite (yet distorted) quotes from Richard Bach's "Jonathan Livingston Seagull."

The dream of flight: The ethereal feeling of falling when you're wrapped in dreams. Perhaps that was one of the motivations that faced a land-locked journalist: writing and presenting the news while dreaming of flight.

Later, Bach and I would become kindred spirits in the sky. I was honored to be mentioned as his "mentor" in skydiving!

Did you ever have one of those days when nothing seems to go right? No matter which lane you're in (on the highway or in the grocery store), it moves the slowest. The teller for whom you're next in line suddenly breaks for lunch! You know, no matter what you do, it isn't right.

Well, you don't want to be skydiving, driving a racecar or disarming a bomb on one of those days. We've all had those kinds of days. Mine was at Cypress Gardens, among the first great tourist attractions in Florida. It is now Legoland. I was skydiving on that hot summer day and nothing seemed to go right for me, except one thing: I lived! Seems a small accomplishment but I lived after falling for more than three thousand feet, when both parachutes failed to open.

Many people ask, "What broke your fall?" I simply reply straight forward, "The ground!" In fact, few people can add definitive proof to the adage, "Of three thousand feet of fall, it's only the last inch that hurt." It's not the

Point of impact — Cypress Gardens, Florida

fall; it's that sudden stop! I suppose I really got Richard Bach interested in the sport of skydiving! He was one of the first to visit me in the hospital in Winter Haven, Florida.

After my transfer to a Tampa Hospital, another close friend, the late Floyd Glisson (former Vice President of Eckerd Drugs) saw to it that a fresh beer

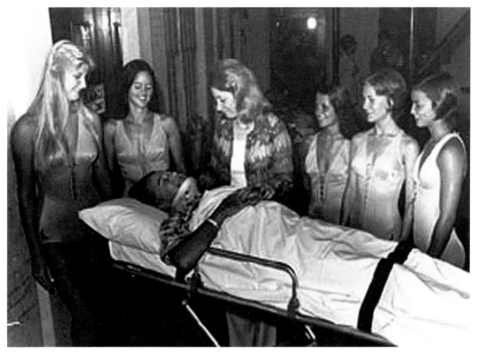

Wife #2, Lillian, and my "nurses"

was delivered to my hospital bed every night! It was not exactly what the doctor ordered but it was very nice indeed! After all, I was much later to become a corporate spokesman for Miller Brewing. Floyd also came to be a "close friend in the sky" as well as on the ground!

Perhaps more amazing is how this country boy from North Carolina, always shy and introverted, came to be in a parachute harness. Moreover, how did he, with this timidity and a supposed speech impediment, come to be a television news anchor in the nation's 14th largest TV market? The two are actually connected. One led to the other.

Almost everyone at some time or another has awakened in a cold sweat, having dreamed of falling through space while at the same time falling from the bed. The fear of falling is apparently an innate part of all of us. It is one of the fears from within. Perhaps it is fear of the unknown. It is a fear that this reporter came to know firsthand. Oh, not that I didn't have the same nighttime dreams about falling. Rather, I was fortunate enough to experience that thrill firsthand.

Chapter 2
How It All Started

As a child I had my head in the sky most of the time...dreaming of being a greater ace, then the many exploits of Walter Mitty. Perhaps hundreds of classroom hours flew past as a young boy daydreamed about having his hands on the controls of a hot fighter plane. It was reflected in his less than stellar grades.

In spite of those daydreams, I somehow made it through high school and college before I began to experience the thrill of flying. Coincidentally, I also fell in love with broadcasting, the thrill of riding another type of air: the airwaves. It provided a lot of satisfaction and a sense of accomplishment. It's not illegal, immoral or fattening! Recently, I saw a bumper sticker that stated: "Remember when sex was safe and sky diving was dangerous?"

As a kid, I was known as the shy guy of the class. For the one with a presumed speech impediment, this was really an accomplishment. After all, except for NBC's former anchorman Tom Brokaw, I was one of the few to make it into the ranks of anchormen without the ability to say "three." Perhaps my teachers thought it was cute or maybe the ABC's and 'rithmetic were more important. (Apparently arithmetic and spelling are no longer paramount in our schools). I avoided the word (or number)! How I got rid of that problem and how I became a broadcaster is another story; but it does involve SEX.

Actually I started out in electronics, taking apart radio and television sets and putting them back together. I had much more success in taking them apart than in reassembling them.

As a would-be engineer, I came in contact with an entrepreneur in my little hometown of Hickory, North Carolina (we'll call him Sam). Sam had his eye on making money in public address broadcasting. It was back in the time when people flocked to see even Class B baseball. This, I believe, was double 'A.' Seems Sam needed a young guy to handle the sound gear for his PA broadcasts. It meant lugging a lot of equipment and running the controls. As long as it didn't require any appearance in front of the microphone or having to speak into it, things were OK. We had a pretty good working relationship. Sam would announce the games while sitting with a pretty young girl and I would handle the controls.

As fate would have it, one night about the seventh inning Sam appeared ill. In fact he began to perspire so heavily I thought he would actually sweat. Suddenly, he looked at me in desperation and shouted "take over!" "Me? You don't mean me in front of the microphone, no way." Sporting a high fever and an unsteady hand, Sam, with young lassie in tow, headed across the roof of the building and shakily down a flimsy wooden ladder.

Suddenly I was alone (much the same as being alone in a haunted house at midnight). Just me and my chrome Shure Microphone... a remnant of the 50's...the type you would always see in the hands of the King, Elvis Presley! It was up to me. What would happen if number "FREE" (3) came to bat. What if he gets FREE strikes or FREE balls on him... or, if he grounds out to the FIRD (third) baseman?! Even worse, what if the Fird Baseman's number is FIRDY-FREE? Man, what a predicament.

Not since the days of Mudville or the strike out of Mighty Casey did the people of Hickory hear such a pitiable announcer.

Sam, however, was the sympathetic sort. He learned of my speech oddity from almost everybody in my little hometown. You know, little hometowns live on gossip! That's not a slam at Hickory. It was and is a wonderful part of North Carolina, in the Piedmont Section. I was grown before I realized the French influence in the Carolinas! Piedmont is French for "foot mountains."

Sam and I talked for a while and in a few minutes, he taught me what no other teacher had even bothered to attempt, how to roll my r's! With a lot of practice, I got better. It was the only direction I could go.

Amazingly, I overcame some of my shyness. I had to, because the malady that stuck Sam seemed to be reoccurring. Fortunately, the young lady stuck by his side like a pilot fish.

Almost every night at the game, about the same time, Sam would begin to breathe heavily! He'd shove the microphone to me and, dashing down the ladder, away he'd go.

One night, I discovered the apparent cause of Sam's strange malady. While running some cables under the announce booth, I couldn't help but notice the blonde's hand provocatively resting on Sam's thigh. As the game progressed, so did the movement of her hand. Inevitably, Sam was beginning to overheat and was racing from the game!

The season ended and Sam went on his way to another, more profitable, business. Never did know what happened to the blonde. That was my entrance into the field of broadcasting.

I always tell people that it was SEX that got me into broadcasting. If the two lovebirds had been more patient or had enjoyed baseball more, I would never have wound up as a television anchor. More likely, I probably wouldn't have wound up in a citrus grove beside an old, mature Grapefruit tree. Thanks Sam, you started me on a wonderful ride! (Sam's name was changed to protect the guilty!)

Chapter 3
The 'Early' Days of Radio

A much younger Arch at the mike

Working in some capacity on the radio was something I considered with much trepidation. The little house of horrors for this timid soul was a local radio station (WHKY, Hickory, NC). Walking in with all the confidence a little boy could muster, like wandering at midnight through a graveyard, the first specter was the station manager. Tall, gaunt and without emotion, he produced a raft of papers gleaned from the wires of the Associated Press. "Here, read this," he commanded, pointing to an ancient WEBCOR wire recorder and a microphone. Reading this (while pretending to be Walter Winchell or some other great air personality) was not without great difficulty. Then came the glare of the station manager who commanded, "Listen to this!" It was not a pretty sound: an awkward kid trying to sound like an experienced air personality. Even worse was the admonition from the station manager, "Would you hire this person?"

Thoroughly humiliated, the kid (like a scolded puppy with his tail between his legs) somberly trudged out the door, never to be seen again, at least not by that station manager.

At that time the first tape recorders were making an appearance nationwide and some entrepreneurs were opening studios where those with supposed confidence could pay to record their voice, either as a singer or a speaker. Now, this was an opportunity waiting to be seized.

Apparently no one truly realizes how their voice sounds to others. Coming out of your own body apparently makes the difference. Once you have heard yourself through recording over and over, one begins to realize how you sound to others. Compiling news stories, make-believe commercials and spending hard-earned money to record announcement and news stories on a Brush tape recorder was a good start!

Finally, with enough unwarranted confidence. this novice announcer tried to get into another radio station. WSIC in Statesville, NC was willing to give a beginner a rare chance. It seems no one would hire someone who had no experience. You couldn't get experience unless you could first get a job in broadcasting. It was a "Catch 22."

Most of the news reporters and announcers were hired strictly by the depth of their voice and mine was yet to fully mature. Now, with the conglomerate corporations that own more than a thousand stations, it is even more difficult to break into broadcasting. The jobs are fewer and harder to get but my break finally came. It meant getting up at 3:30 every weekday morning and trying to act awake at sign-on time (5AM), sometimes coming straight from a late night date. It also gave this announcer time to squeeze in courses at Mitchell College in Statesville. It was a beginning experience that only whetted my appetite for more.

Believing (over-confidently) that I was moving up the ladder of success, I accepted an announcer's position in Rock Hill, SC. It was becoming a difficult time. Not only because I was trying to become a 'hot' air personality but also because I was concerned with some four thousand young ladies encamped at

Winthrop College, located in the small town. So, you see, I had to split my time. After all, I was single. So many beautiful ladies and not enough time! It didn't afford much sleeping time.

It was a time in which "Bebop" was making the rounds in music, well ahead of hip-hop or rap. In fact, one young intern at the station inherited the name "Bebop." It sort of fit with his wavy hair and popularity with the fairer gender. The situation was looking up for awhile but it was in the 50's but things were reaching the boiling point in a section of the world known as Korea.

The military draft was starting up and soon we would hear about battles called "Heartbreak Ridge" and about an almost imaginary parallel which we were not supposed to cross.

I FEEL A DRAFT

As the draft drew closer, I chose the U.S. Air Force. My hat's off to the men and women of the Army, Navy and the Marines but my dreams of flying into combat were not to be. During the first 30-day leave from the Air Force my high school sweetheart, Margaret Lutz, and I were married. Talk about putting off things until the last moment, we got hitched the last day of my leave. Then, it was off to a little base in Arizona while assignments were being passed out. I felt, as many younger people, that I should be flying in Korea. This, however, was not to be.

I was stationed in Southern Germany and enjoyed the countryside, the people, brats, its beer and Rhine wine while others served in the freezing muck that described Korea. I "fought the battle" in Deutschland... learning about their great beers and wines, particularly Liebfraumilch (a white Rhine wine translated loosely as "lover's milk").

Fortunately for me, no North Korean MIGS flew into my area in Southern Germany.

Those who served in that hellhole of Korea could ever have been adequately commended. My brother Charles, also a journalist, probably wished he had been sent to Germany. Instead, as a reporter for the Air Force Times in Korea, he had seen the awful reality of war there; particularly when he had to rapidly withdraw from the Chosen Reservoir from 27 November to 11 December, 1950. Battling desperately night and day in the face of almost insurmountable odds, throughout a period of two weeks of intense and sustained combat, the

First Marine Division, reinforced, emerged from its ordeal as a fighting unit with its wounded, its guns and equipment and its prisoners. It had decisively defeated seven enemy divisions. For that, the unit received The Presidential Unit Citation. But the men who were there can tell that story far better than this reporter. To tell a story and to tell it accurately, you had to be there.

After Korea, it was back to work in civilian life and that, of course, was radio. A devout newsman, Ed Smith built a radio station in the little hometown of Hickory. It's an area formerly best known for furniture factories and hosiery mills, along with a host of friendly people. Fresh out of the Air Force, I was added to the staff as an announcer. Such an assignment sounds "romantic" but it had many duties associated with it. Among them was a regular "chewing-out" from Smith if anything went wrong. You must learn early not to throw gasoline on a raging fire.

Not yielding to such a temptation, Smith would come back later to apologize for the loss of temper and things would be back to normal (for a while).

BACK TO SCHOOL

At the same time, this reporter was back at the books at Lenoir-Rhyne College, a small warm and friendly center of learning in Hickory. It has since become a University. Deciding to finish college as rapidly as possible and to keep the tax-free GI Bill checks flowing in, I carried 18 semester hours constantly while working a full 40 hours at the radio station. That load was increased when Smith suffered a minor heart attack and had to cut back on his hours. The news assignments were offered to me, increasing my workload to about 60 hours per week while continuing the full college load. It meant getting up at 3:30 every morning and getting to the station at about 5:00. Then, the newsgathering began: calling all the sources, listening to police radio scanners and gleaning the wires of the Associated Press for news. After preparing the news, I presented it at 7:45, ending at 8:00 am, and then dashed across town for the first class at 8 o'clock; of course, I was always late!

The race continued at 11:25 each morning. Leaving class, I would scramble to the apartment that my wife, Margaret, and I shared only several blocks from the college. After gulping down a quick sandwich and giving a kiss to the wife, I raced downtown again to arrive at the station at noon.

That shift continued until 7:00 pm, when I would buzz home for dinner when I was not covering a city council meeting or the like and hit the "sack" by

9:00 or 10:00 each night to be ready for that 3:30 am call the following morning. It was tough but it worked and eventually I got that college degree. By golly, I got it the "old fashioned way." I worked for it.

One morning, a long, lanky kid was pounding on the outer glass of the radio station's studio. This was back before we had to lock the doors and place security guards. With a record in place I went to the door to ask the kid what I could do for him. Well, in his drawling Carolina accent he said, "Ahm (I'm) a student at the University of Nawth Caroliner at Chapel Hill, and I got this here recording I would like you to play." Could you imagine getting a record played today, with the monopoly that a few huge corporations have over radio? "Well," I asked, "what's it about?" Continuing in his heavy drawl he said, "It's 'bout that country boy who's from so far in the hills he ain't seen much of nothin' when he comes upon this rectangular field. Wal…" he continued, "…these men are wearing leather helmets and playing with an oblong-shaped ball, and when it would hit the ground, they would commence to jump on top it! So, I got myself an RC Cola and a Moon Pie and I commenced to watch." What it was was football! So, in a very small way, my playing this first big hit helped launch a multi-million dollar career for ANDY GRIFFITH! I haven't seen him since!

Andy Griffith

I'm not making fun of the North Carolina accent! I was raised there and it took years and years trying to hide the accent to be on the radio. And now, accents are more desirable than ever. How sad it would be if everyone sounded alike. So, don't say anything about rednecks! I used to be one!

North Carolina was the "hotbed" of NASCAR racing! Lots of drivers got their early experience racing down mountain roads at night with questionable cargoes!

During all of this "spare time" between 18-semester hours at college and working 60 hours a week, Margaret and I welcomed our first little one into the world: Karen Theresa. Truly a "bouncing baby," Karen soon had three chins (at least) and controlled the household as babies usually do. Fortunately, considering my early hours, she began to sleep through the night when she was only a month old. Like clockwork, another bundle of joy, in the form of Diane, was born in 1956. She made life more exciting every evening for six months with a bout of old fashioned colic. Nevertheless, she was loved. Karen had great musical talent, apparently a gift from her mother, an accomplished church organist.

In later years, Karen kept me busy chasing the boys away. Her musical talent developed to the extent she played keyboards for a number of bands, eventually playing with the Mod Squad in Tampa. This eventually led her and the band to do a "lead-in" to the famed Jefferson Airplane, with lead singers Marty Balin and Grace Slick. That led to romance, marriage and a sweet little off-spring called Delaney! The history of the Airplane, and later the Starship, was inducted into the Rock and Roll Hall of Fame in 1996.

Marty Balin

Ever wonder how the band got the moniker of "Jefferson Airplane?" An early band member had a dog with that name! Reminds me of a former neighbor who had a dog named Boozer. I passed her on the street one morning as she was calling her dog! "Lose your husband?" I joked! I think I lost a neighbor then!

Actually daughter Diane was to be a TV star before her father. The once very popular Candid Camera show came to Tampa...and dropped in on her kindergarten class. The kids were to paint their names on a glass pane, while the TV crew filmed from the other side. Diane strode to the glass, and quickly painted D-A-N-E ..... then with tongue in cheek, painted in the missing 'I' and dotted it.

Chapter 5
TV Beckons

It was not long before the opportunities and excitement of moving up in the radio field came to me. It was an offer to move to the so-called "Queen City" of Charlotte, NC. The money was tempting and the larger metropolitan market beckoned! The station, WIST in Charlotte, was to be another stepping stone. In my sight was the new medium of television. It was fascinating and, of course, "everybody" watched the little dots trying to act like people.

By that time Margaret and I had two little ones to care for: Karen, who was our first-born in 1953; and Diane who followed in 1956. I was, and remain, a very proud papa of my little girls. We enjoyed Charlotte, hoping a television position would soon become available. It wasn't all that far away. It was in the hyphenated city called Winston-Salem, NC, home to most major cigarette manufacturers. There, we had the "very rich" (mostly in tobacco) and the "little people" who largely lived in the Moravian section (Salem). The station was WSJS-TV, named for its owners the Winston-Salem Journal Sentinel.

We moved into a four-room rental house that was complete with knotty pine paneling throughout. Margaret, the kids and I unloaded the dozens of boxes of our possessions and headed for dinner at a local restaurant. Coming back less than two hours later, we entered the rental house and turned on the lights. You can't imagine our consternation as we viewed tens of thousands of German roaches all over the walls. Apparently, the grooves for the knotty pine gave them a great hiding place. They were everywhere and already infiltrating the boxes we had unloaded. We went to a motel and moved out the next day. After a bout with German roaches, I would look forward to the Florida Palmetto bugs.

WSJS-TV was an invaluable training ground. Between catching glimpses of the "big ones," Arlene Francis and a young kid named Hugh Downs in the morning, I got the opportunity to do everything. That not only meant doing the newscasts but the sports and weather as well. Talk shows were part of the job and between those more appealing tasks, I found myself running the video cameras or striking a set. As I said, it was a great training ground.

From the beginning, I had my sights on a new TV station that was about to be awarded to contenders in Charlotte, NC. My hopes and contacts were with an impresario named Larry Walker. He told me that when his group got the FCC approval, I would be back with the new station in Charlotte.

It was only a short six months when the nod was given: Walker, a former vaudevillian with a charismatic charm, got the approval and my little family was on the way back to Charlotte where a frantic pace was undertaken to get the station on the air.

To hasten the target date, a studio was added to the transmitter building far out of the sprawling Queen City of Charlotte in Mecklenburg County. When I say far out, it really was! It was a drive in the country every morning getting to the TV station.

Unfortunately, migrating flocks of birds were not informed that a huge TV tower was erected in their flight path. One morning when it was foggy, it was a very sad sight to see all the once-winged creatures dotting the landscape around the TV tower. It was, for many of them, their last migration. It was especially sad for one who loves to fly!

Soon the new station had a grand opening and invited the townspeople of Charlotte to come and see the new facilities. We took turns touring the visitors about the station. I noticed one quiet gentleman standing alone with no one offering to give a tour. I eagerly showed him around the studios and found him to be a very pleasant person. Later, I was told I had just given the tour to the owner of the station.

Charlotte was another great training ground. I worked with many well-known Charlotte personalities like Jimmy Kilgo, Jack Callaghan and rubbed shoulders with some of the greats from our competitor, WBT radio and television, like Clyde "Cloudy" McLain and Arthur Smith.

Then I received an opportunity to further my career by moving south to Tampa, Florida. Eugene Dodson, Manager of WTVT in Tampa, vacationed in the Carolina Hills and made me an offer: Come to Florida!

THE EARLY ANCHOR DAYS

I had reached the point where I was television anchorman at a station in one of the nation's major TV markets, the Metroplex of Tampa-St Petersburg, Florida. It has become obvious to me over the years that most viewers feel the television anchorman really is the person who has it made. After all, all they have to do is walk into the studio five minutes before the newscast, glance over a prepared script, then read it from a teleprompter. Actually, part of that has become the custom over the past few years, but in its infancy, funny things could and did often happen. I found out early I had to know the story, and keep a copy in front of me… just in case the 'prompter died or the teleprompter operator fell asleep at the control! Yes, that did happen to me, fortunately only once, but it was enough to get my attention.

As Margaret was in Tampa General Hospital with our newborn son, Douglas Jeffrey, I was onboard the "Jose Gaspar," a steel, flat-bottom pirate ship used every year to recreate the Gasparilla invasion of Tampa. It was totally unseaworthy but an important part of the Gasparilla celebration! Each year leading business professionals of Tampa dress up in full pirate regalia, complete with make-believe scars, to "loot" the city. The parade is perhaps only second to the Mardi Gras (Fat Tuesday) and draws hundreds of thousands of spectators to the Tampa waterfront. Finding myself on board that pirate ship, unfortunately, I didn't have the presence of mind to bring earplugs! The blast of the cannon and blank-loaded six guns left a permanent impression and a temporary, but monumental headache.

It may be more than a coincidence but shortly before my son was born, I met with the "then" hot CBS newsman Douglas Edwards. Should my son become an anchor some day, he would have an effective name: Douglas Deal. At least it sounded good.

My name was always a problem! My full name is Archie. All I needed was a Veronica. Actually I had a lady friend named Veronica for a short while…. but that's another story. I was often called "R.G. Steel." It really didn't help much when I shortened it to Arch. It just seemed a little more formal for TV news. Even then, some called me Art Steel.

It wasn't long afterwards that Shari Lynne was born, the fourth Deal in our family. The growing family truly kept me and Margaret busy. Television journalism proved to be a job that required all of my energy and resources. While searching for news, and a different angle on the news, you're constantly battling the rating wars. A few points down and you are history! I always kept in mind the guy sweeping the floors probably wanted my job and he probably feels he could do it better.

Always, I've considered a news reporter's job was to report the news, nothing more, nothing less. We all can have an "off" day. It happens to quarterbacks and wide receivers. Even so, no matter how lousy you feel, or if the wife fussed at you and your dog bit you, you still must do the same job every day. Nobody cares that you've had a bad day. As an adjunct professor, teaching television years later at Hillsborough Community College in Tampa, I always tried to instill this principle into my students. In fact, viewers deserve a factual, honest news presentation, not a medical review on the sort of day you may have had!

Imagine, however, that you're reporting the news while a 20-foot-long Anaconda snake is wrestling with two handlers and apparently the Anaconda is winning the battle. This happened live on Channel 38 from the St. Petersburg Pier, also known at that time as "The Million Dollar Pier." Burl McCarty, affectionately known as Captain Mac, was ending his children's show that led up to my news broadcast. The huge reptile was pulled from its sack and box but apparently wasn't too happy about it. Someone had forgotten to feed the

gargantuan creature, which apparently was making dinner plans: two handlers and a news reporter.

Trying to act totally nonchalant, I continued with the news as the two men were being drawn together by the huge reptile. It was a sight indeed, but somehow the two were able to get the serpent back into the sack without loss of life or arms.

Burl (Captain Mac) McCarty

Actually the only injury was to the Anaconda. In attempting to bite one of the handlers, it slashed itself. And so the news continued.

McCarty always carried a 38 revolver by his side. However, the end of the barrel was bent from a long hard drop and would not have fired anyway. Worse yet, it could have blown up in his hands. Maybe that's why he never used it!

Among the most memorable things about this business are the people I worked with and the people I met. Journalists meet presidents, movie stars and the like, as a part of our job. And mind you, it's not one we complain about.

My assignment had me set to interview academy award winner William Holden (Sunset Boulevard) at Busch Gardens in Tampa. Halfway through the interview, my cameraman ran out of film (we used 16mm film in those days). As he returned to the news vehicle to fetch more, Holden suggested we take a stroll and enjoy the scenery. Here I was, walking with this great actor when we passed two ladies. One

William Holden

blurted to the other, "Oh, look, that's Arch Deal!" I could have melted into the cement from embarrassment. Here I, a lowly news reporter, am walking with a famous actor and the ladies didn't even notice him. Holden laughed and said, "This is your territory…they wouldn't expect to see me here!" He chuckled at my humbled countenance and we continued on our way. That was the sort of guy he was!.

After my first successful year as a news anchor, I was honored by two of America's top cartoonists, Fred Laswell, the creator of Snuffy Smith

(who lived and drew the cartoons in Tampa) and Chic Young, the creator of Dagwood and Blondie (who lived in Clearwater, west of Tampa). They honored me with these cartoons:

To COUSIN ARCH – MANY HAPPY RETURNS – FRED LASSWELL

Skydiving into the famed Brick Yard in Indianapolis was a true delight and an honor…especially when I got to land beside famed actor James Garner. He was chosen several times to be the grand marshal for the pre-race parade. When I landed next to him, I was amazed by the charm and grace of this actor, who gave me a hug when I landed. We traded a few comments on the microphone and I left the track. A year later, he was again standing on the track when I landed my Miller canopy.

"Arch," he asked, "are you still skydiving?" "Sure, Jim," I replied! "Are you still making movies?" What a guy! Years later, I would get a chance to say basically the same thing to John Elway, two-time Super Bowl Champion on one

James Garner

of my dozen leaps into the famed Mile-High Stadium. "Arch, you still sky diving?" "John, you still playing football?" As a Miller Lite All Star, I had the pleasure of skydiving into the old Mile High Stadium 12 times... always landing on the 50 yard line or thereabouts. This I truly loved. It was a very difficult jump, opening your parachute over a mile and a half above the Mile High Stadium in the thin air, aiming for the center of the field. The fans were fabulous and supportive of their Broncos.

Actually, my first jump into that stadium was for the first USFL (United States Football League) Super Bowl. It was on a very hot July day. The temperature was 100 degrees which, in terms of density altitude, put the stadium, in theory, about 9,500 feet above sea level. Remarkably, I performed a stand-up landing. Then came the hard part: I would gather up my parachute, wave to the crowd and start the climb up the very steep stairs to the top. Along the way, the enthusiastic crowd provided me with hundreds of "high fives" until I reached the very top rim of the stadium. Man that was really tiring! But it was so much fun!

One of dozens of stadium jumps

Chapter 6
Bill Henry

Among the people I had the pleasure of working with in the Tampa television market was Bill Henry. He came from reporting the racial conflicts of Montgomery, Alabama, to the Tampa market. A true journalist, Bill was a no-nonsense man. Comments and words that commonly get on the air today would never pass the critical eye of Bill Henry. A hard-working, dedicated family man and church deacon, he received the respect of all who served with him. But even though words were carefully chosen, Bill found there would be at least two words he would never use again in news stories.

The first came about when he reported on the successful biological experiment launched on a space rocket from Cape Canaveral. "Today," Bill announced in the newscast, "a living orgasm was launched into space!"

Another incident came when he was reporting the apprehension of a thug by the Hillsborough County Sheriff's Department. "As the suspect was being led to the cell, he suddenly seized one of the deputy's guns. But, before he could use it, both deputies jumped on top of the man and seduced him." Bill added, "Anyway, he had head injuries." "Orgasm" and "Seduced": two words that Bill studiously avoided in the future. Still, Bill Henry received and deserved the respect of all!

To me, it seems one of the best ways to keep your ratings up is (in addition to presenting the best darn newscast in the area) to keep yourself visible to the public. If news happens, be there.   If there isn't any news, create it.

You create "news" by developing a human-interest story or finding a way to tell the story the others forgot.

Using this system got this reporter patrolling off the Cuban coast in a U.S. Navy submarine during the Cuban Missile Crisis, getting too close on a NATO maneuver off the coast of Greece and digging into a foxhole while bombs and machine gun fire rattled much too close to me.

When General Fulgencio Batista's regime began to crumble in the land of clear Havana Cigars, Fidel Castro's rebels, along with Che Guevara, began to take control. Whatever truly happened to Guevara, a devout communist, remains a mystery... except perhaps to Fidel, who could have found himself playing second fiddle.

Then came the Cuban Missile Crisis.

The crisis really started on January 1, 1959, when Fidel Castro officially took control of Cuba after leading a successful revolt against Batista.

**Arch and ace producer Bob Gilbert readying
for trip to Guantanamo Bay, Cuba**

In October of 1959, the U.S. began setting up 15 nuclear-tipped Jupiter missiles along Turkey's border with the Soviet Union. Days later, Soviet Premier Khrushchev recommended the deployment of similar Soviet missiles in Cuba.

Given Castro's bent to become a Soviet-style communist leader favored by Khrushchev, relations between Cuba and the US went downhill. We tried and failed to kill Castro, we tried and failed to invade Castro's island at the Bay of Pigs and by early 1961, had cut off all trade and diplomatic relations with Castro.

We probably should have known something bad was at hand on October 8, 1962, when Cuban President Dorticós told the General Assembly of the United Nations, "If we (Cuba) are attacked, we will defend ourselves. I repeat, we have sufficient means with which to defend ourselves; we have indeed our inevitable weapons, the weapons which we would have preferred not to acquire and which we do not wish to employ."

What did Dorticós mean by "inevitable weapons"?

Early in the morning of October 14, 1962, U.S. Air Force Major Richard Heyser found out when cameras inside his U2 spy plane took pictures of Soviet medium-range ballistic missile (MRBM) sites being constructed in Cuba.

Having applied months before, this reporter was among the first local newscasters to be allowed back into the eastern tip of Cuba: Oriente Province and Guantanamo Bay. Tension there was very heavy as the U.S. prepared to go to war over the placement of missiles in Cuba. Flying the defense perimeter in the so-called "no-man's land" that separated the rest of Cuba from the U.S. base at Guantanamo, some of the missile sites could be seen from the air. Also visible was the flurry of activity to dismantle the sites and float them back to Russia.

Preparing for the talk-up (locking the camera into position, then standing in front of it to deliver the story), I ventured into the "demilitarized zone" of Cuba, an area between Castro's Cuba and the U.S. Naval Base at Guantanamo Bay. There I stood and delivered my story as a Cuban gunman on Castro's side nervously played with his Russian-supplied automatic weapon. If he was trying to make me nervous, he certainly succeeded. Trying to conceal that fact in my delivery, I finished the talk-up and sauntered back to the safety of the U.S. side.

It's really a beautiful island, covered on that Eastern end with Bougainvillea and wild orchids. It's a shame it went from a dictator like Batista (working with mob bosses who ran the casinos) to a communist dictator who never let anyone threaten his power, who crushed the little people and maintained his hold over Cuba.

I am fortunate to have many Hispanic friends in Tampa and I do love my Café con Leche and Medianoches! (Translation: Cuban coffee with milk and midnight sandwiches, a Cuban sandwich on egg bread.) Tampa has many Hispanic restaurants ranging from the famous Columbia Restaurant to great coffee and Cuban sandwich shops like La Ideal. In fact, Tampa was once called the Cigar City, since it housed dozens of cigar factories. Many have moved north where cigars are machine rolled. The great ones now come from Honduras, Nicaragua and Guatemala, since the importation of Cuban Cigars in the U.S. is illegal.

The Caribbean rollers of fine cigars raise the tobacco from Cuban seed and import them all over the world. Not one to ever touch a cigarette, I find myself sorely tempted occasionally to smoke a premium cigar. After all, I was living and growing up in the "Cigar City."

For the next month, we watched Kennedy, Castro and Khrushchev play "Truth or Dare" with our lives. But everything worked out fine. Castro sent the missiles back to Khrushchev. Decades later and after a long hassle and controversy, we sent Elian Gonzales (the boy at the center of the much publicized immigration controversy) back to Castro.

Chapter 7
Salute and Farewell to Walter

Tampa is just across the Florida Peninsula from Cape Canaveral, where America's astronauts rocketed into space three different times with the goal of eventually landing on the moon. We in the news industry looked forward to observing and reporting on each of these fantastic events. There were also dozens of shorter manned flights.

Walter Cronkite

Many times I traveled across the state to witness and report these events. As a newsman, I would gather all my materials and practice the stand-up narration of the events about to happen. During one of the Apollo missions, I found a small deserted shed where I would practice: "This is Arch Deal reporting from Cape Canaveral, where Apollo 11 is about to be launched..." "click... rrrr... click... rrr... click..." the sound of a motorized 35-millimeter camera made me stop and turn to see from where it was coming. "Sorry to disturb you, I'm just taking some pictures of the Cape for my grandchildren." The voice unmistakably was that of Walter Cronkite!

In the television news industry, as in most news gathering organizations, there is competition to "get it first.... but first, get it right." Walter was the main, and I do mean major, competitor in the network news business. He had been named "The most trusted man in America." That honor came—not from the network—but from the American audience. No matter what went wrong in the world, everything would be all right... because Walter was there. Of course, I respected the man and had a very short but well remembered chat with the "elder statesman of television." Later, Walter left and I resumed my practice talk-up prior to launch.

Walter Cronkite further polished the image. I always had respect and admiration for the CBS competitor.

At least two years later, I had the occasion to visit New York City. Usually I would go to take in a Broadway show. Months earlier, WFLA-TV meteorologist Gordon Barnes was offered the opportunity to move to the Big Apple and report the weather for CBS-Television.

Gordon invited me to visit him in the CBS Newsroom. We were competitors but good friends as well.

As Gordon was showing me around the newsroom, he spied Walter Cronkite gathering copy from the wire machines. Gordon said "I've got to introduce you to Walter Cronkite." Quickly he strode up to Mr. Cronkite and said, "Mr. Cronkite, I would like to introduce you to..." but before he could finish Cronkite said, "Oh, I remember Arch Deal, we met at Cape Canaveral at one of the launches." Gordon and I were flabbergasted. This is another tribute to the man: Cronkite remembered people and remembered where he had met them! I was both humbled and honored that he had this remarkable ability to recall so vividly the people he met... and where he met them. Again, the praise is to this honored giant in the news reporting business. We may never see another of his caliber but it should inspire young reporters to aspire to his professionalism! As Walter would say, "And that's the way it is."

Chapter 8
Submarine Duty

Another assignment sent this reporter off the Coast of Cuba in a Guppy Snorkel Submarine to watch activity along the Cuban coastline. In accomplishing this, I would feel what it's like to live under water for months at a time (in a nuclear sub). They have to be a gregarious sort to rub shoulders with fellow crewmen who are in your face day and night.

This was a World War II class sub: no huge compartments here, just tight, tight living. I found myself submerged days on end with no daylight and incredible tightness. You learn to get along with your neighbor. After all, you're in the same boat together.

As a newsman, I felt tremendous drama aboard the sub. During a normal day, if there is anything normal about a sub, it is a very noisy world. When they decide to dive, the klaxon horns sound and the Captain commands, "Dive…Dive…Dive!" There is no doubt about the intentions. The rush of water fills the sub's ballast tanks and the nose of the sub dives into the blue waters of the Gulf of Mexico and is soon plunged in the depths, completely out of sight.

What a picture this would make!

What an idea! I talked to the captain and he agreed to let me leave the sub, in the middle of the Gulf, and photograph the crash dive of the Guppy Snorkel Sub. Then I would record the sudden "porpoise out of the water" affecting an emergency surface so that the sub could prepare to fire the ship's exterior guns (or just assent in case of a catastrophe!).

In the tiny rubber raft, I was set adrift in the vast expanse of the Gulf to photograph the sub's remarkable ability to suddenly engulf its tanks with water and disappear beneath the now tranquil ocean. What a beautiful sight! Then, all was silent, terrible silence and a rapid feeling of being all alone in the middle of the expanse of blue water. To really know loneliness…find yourself in the middle of an expanse of open ocean, over 30 miles from land.

The silence and the wait were interminable. The captain knew what he was doing. He made me wait…and wait….and wait…wondering if they would ever return to rescue this newsman who was beginning to wonder what the heck he was doing way out here.

Just as sudden and more exciting was the appearance of the bow of the sub, zooming out of the water like a homesick flying fish. The massive steel hull crashed back down sending cascading plumes of water and mist into the formerly serene Gulf. It was beautiful and reassuring to see the sub back on the surface. And more important, I was about to be "rescued." The appearance of the sub was a beautiful sight to behold.

Soon I was back on board, acting like it was nothing unusual. I now feel all the crewmen were in on the joke on the newsman but I did get some spectacular footage for my story.

Once onboard, I filmed the same sequence from the interior of the sub, complete with the klaxon horns and the command to "Dive, Dive, Dive."

My hat's off to the submariners: They are indeed a very special breed! I honor them—from afar! I'll stick to skydiving! We have an agreement with sharks: Don't come up here and we won't bother you down there!

Chapter 9
Wild Stunts

Realizing it had captured the fancy of the viewers and myself as well, I decided to delve deeper in reporting the activities of the military people around Tampa and St. Petersburg. After all the area was home to a wing of the Tactical Air Command, which flew regular sorties carrying nuclear weapons during the Cold War, the United States Strike Command (Swift Tactical Reaction in Every Known Environment) that headquartered the decision makers during both Gulf wars, and the US Central Command, which was the home base for operations during the Iraq and Afghanistan Wars.

The opportunities to cover events surrounding action at MacDill Air Force Base, sometimes called Fort MacDill, were immense. One of my wildest, craziest stunts was sitting atop a napalm bomb while conducting an interview with the technician who was disarming the device. The EOD expert said it wouldn't help to be a hundred yards away, "If you're within a hundred yards, it'll get you anyway." Foolishly, instead of heading for the hills, I just sat on the bomb while he calmly disarmed it. Thinking back, I cannot imagine a more stupid act for anyone to commit. Perhaps I should have been "committed." He was one very cool character and he found an unwitting news reporter dumb enough to sit atop a napalm bomb. Imagine, I used to say, "My mom didn't raise any idiots!" I should have kept quiet.

Following coverage of Vietnam, with no new exciting battle scenes to film, I turned my attention to fighter jet deployment.

Taking part in television news had many benefits besides money, which honestly was very meager at the time. Among the benefits was being able to "rub shoulders" with world leaders.

The United States Strike Command, headquartered at MacDill Air Force Base on the southern peninsula of Tampa, invited this newsman to accompany them on an exercise to cover the NATO (North Atlantic Treaty Organization) countries. The trip encompassed traveling from MacDill to Cannon Air Force Base in Clovis, New Mexico, and flying non-stop from there in an F-100 Super Saber jet to Turkey. Now, this was my cup of tea.

Always the pilot, (and even as a little kid, a pilot wannabe) I relished this opportunity, 12 hours of sitting in an ejection seat was the plan, with at least six air-to-air refuelings en route. This picture shows me boarding an F4 Phantom. Later "Speedy Pete" Everette, who wrote The Fastest Man Alive, totally wore me out.

But it was like throwing Br'er Rabbit into the briar patch. With over 20,000 hours of commercial pilot time to my credit, this was a dream assignment. The task wasn't that simple at all. Many hours of briefing were required before we ate a good-sized dinner and settled down to get some "sack time." Then, another briefing was scheduled prior to beginning that long flight from New Mexico to Dezful, Iran. One stop over had been planned at Incirlik, Turkey, the site of Gary Powers' infamous flight in the U-2 Spy Plane over Russia. Just north of that area, his aircraft was brought down by a surface-to-air missile (one of the earliest SAMs). Powers safely parachuted to earth where his Russian captors imprisoned him until a spy exchange bought his freedom. Unfortunately, Powers was later to fatally crash his helicopter in Los Angeles while flying for traffic reports. Sometimes, as I would discover later, flying traffic can be almost as deadly as missiles. But that's another chapter.

Our take off from Cannon AFB was not without incident. One of the aircraft malfunctioned on takeoff and had to return to base, leaving one highly disappointed pilot who would be destined to be wide awake for the next day or two.

Flying through the night across America, our flight of F-100s constantly ran into thunderstorms, the types that toss you about the sky like so much flotsam on the water. The air, charged with electricity, always produced a huge flash of static electricity as we attempted to mate the probe of our F-100 with the drogue of the KC-135 tanker aircraft. Like taking a tiger by the tail, we whipped about the sky but somehow managed to hang on long enough to take fuel and continue our long trek. That system has since been improved with a hard contact probe into the feeding jet's fuel system. Still, it takes a monumental amount of piloting skill to line up the probe and take on the necessary fuel. Either you get fueled, or your flight is about to suddenly come to an end. These multi-million dollar jets are thirsty boogers!

There was more preparation prior to crossing the very cold Northern Atlantic. We wore what were unaffectionately called "Poopy Suits." Heavy rubberized canvas, they proved to be great for weight-loss through evaporation. Heavy plastic rings about the wrists and the neck provided the only outlet for air that was pumped into the suits from a navel-like fitting. The object, should you have to eject from the aircraft over the Atlantic, was to give you a minute or two longer to get into the life raft before you are totally incapacitated by the freezing cold. On the way down, under a parachute, you were instructed to roll the sleeves forward and roll the neck up to seal out the frigid water. Putting on the suits, especially around the wrists, was a great way to remove hair from your forearm and wrists. It works better than a depilatory… but it's a lot more painful. Without this protection, you would only have scant seconds to board the life raft before the cold would make it impossible to help yourself.

It did its job! I felt like I lost about five pounds on that crossing. It was all water weight, which I would put back on as soon as I got to a cold beer (or two).

The ejection seat, upon which I had to sit up to 12 hours at a time, cannot be padded. If in an emergency you had to eject, the cushioning would serve to crush your spine. The incredibly rapid rate of acceleration would allow the cushion to suddenly deflate, with the force striking you right in the butt, perhaps leading to crushed vertebrae. Therefore, you grin and bear it. After hours and hours of flight, your bottom becomes increasingly uncomfortable then, thankfully, begins to numb. When your posterior becomes totally numb it's a blessing. You don't want to awaken your posterior, lest the pain returns.

Over the Mediterranean, we ran into more storms. The wildly gyrating probe and drogue refueling technique managed to unscrew the head from one of the probes, forcing a pilot in our cell to abort and land on a tiny island off the Italian Coast (on which the U.S. had a support base).

Flying into the U.S. Airbase at Incirlik, in Southeast Turkey was a welcome relief. Incirlik Air Base is located about 7.5 miles east of Adana. Incirlik was home of the 39th Air Base Wing. Incirlik provides vital support for 21 units, including the squadrons of the 39th Mission Support Group. Adana, with a population of over one million, is the fourth largest city in Turkey.

As we taxied into position and shut down the burner on the Super Saber, a crewman climbed up the side and offered me a cold beer. That was most welcome. Getting up and out of the ejection seat was more difficult than you could imagine. My entire southern exposure was numb and didn't respond well to motion. Nonetheless, I somehow climbed down the ladder of my aluminum steed and felt like an astronaut must feel when he returns to earth, with one exception. With the absence of gravity, I think they escape the sore posterior problem. Next was the job of getting out of the "Poopy Suit."

Actually, I think they sort of poured me out of the suit. It looked as if my flight had been in a sauna! In spite of my sore bottom, I found myself in the Officers Club, seated and swapping "war stories" with my fellow aviators.

At the crack of dawn we were up and out of there, again kicking the tires and lighting the fires on our F100s. Next stop Teheran.

I had heard that the dust storms sometimes kick up in Iran, sending clouds of talcum-powder-thin duty soaring as high as 50 thousand feet into the sky. Sounds impossible, I thought. I was soon to be proved wrong. As our cell of fighter jets passed closed to Iraq and into the territory of Iran, we ran into those impenetrable dust storms. Amazingly, we found visibility was almost zero. Carefully watching our altitude and separation, each jet began the spiral downward for landing, penetrating deeper and deeper into the orange dust. I could almost feel the fighter in front of us and wondered about the one behind us. Deeper and deeper into the gloom we descended, hoping not to become part of the landscape. Lacking great navigational gear, we were being "talked down" by GCA (Ground Control Approach).

"Okay, Saber 111, you're a little high and right of the runway, bring it on down…" This was the approach chatter until we felt the bump of asphalt under our tires. Only a split second before touchdown could the runway be seen. The dust was so thick it was hazardous to taxi. Nevertheless, we had made it all the way from Cannon AFB in New Mexico to Tehran. And that, I thought, was an accomplishment! As always, my hat's off to the men and women of the U.S. Air Force. Flying those missions brought home the sacrifices and integrity of our pilots. They all love to fly, and in doing so, always protect America.

Dodging Bullets and Bombs

Imagine sitting atop a hill overlooking the Aegean Sea. Below, to the north was Solonika (Thessaloniki); Salonika is a strategically important Greek port on the Aegean coast of Macedonia, as there is a direct railway link between Salonika and Belgrade, Yugoslavia. Salonika featured fabulous Greek foods, feta cheese and, of course, Metaxa (a blend of brandy and wine that would make a great charcoal lighter fluid).

The United States Strike Command had scheduled a major land-sea exercise on this lush beachfront and all I had to do (along with a dozen other news reporters) was watch from the high vantage point, and sip tea with King Constantine, then the king of Greece.

All of this was, of course, breathtaking; but the action, the real meat of the story, was down on the beachhead. Imagine filming the troops storming ashore after the shelling from the battleships far out in the Aegean. The most exciting point would be watching the landing craft run aground on the sand, the bow doors flopping downward, and the troops racing through the shallow water to simulate taking the beachhead. Luckily, I was able to commandeer a jeep and drive down the mountain to the beachhead. The pounding by the heavy 8-inch guns had abated, so now was the time to move. Arriving at a fenced-off area, I stopped the jeep and proceeded past a Greek guard who apparently thought I knew what I was doing (boy, was he wrong!). Racing across the sand, the landing craft were visible far from the beachhead. Great! I had time to make it!

I hadn't counted on one minor little item. After the shelling and before the landing craft hit the beach, the aircraft suddenly appeared aimed at the final softening up of the beach! That "softening up" consisted of strafing and bombing the area one more time. And there I was, right in the center, where no one would want to be, unless they happen to have a death wish. In spite of what you are reading I do not have a death wish!

As the first group of planes swooped in, I frantically dove into a shallow ditch and raced to dig in deeper. No time to film this episode! It could have proved to be "the last film taken by the late newsman!" Amazingly, with all the bullets flying and the bombs bursting, jarring me out of my hiding place and unceremoniously dropping me back in, I was never hit or harmed (although I was covered by sand). As the strafing ended, I emerged from the impromptu shelter and raced for the beach to get the first pictures of the troops charging ashore. Was it worth it? Well, the 16mm footage was great but I definitely would not try that stunt again. And, I didn't want to endure the scolding I would get from General Paul D. Adams (architect of the United States Strike Command) for the stunt. He had the ability to make a bird colonel cry, if they didn't have their facts straight. Therefore, I never told the General anything, unless I was sure of my facts. We seemed to get along very well. He once said, "You outrank all of us; you are a civilian."

Then there was the time that another NATO maneuver was being held. This one was in Iran at a time when they were much friendlier to the U.S. The Shah of Iran was in control and wherever he went the parade route was lined with people. Wherever he walked, he walked on the finest Persian Carpets. One such event was close to Persepolis. Now called Shiraz, it is an ancient and beautiful city. Before the gathered newsmen assembled for the event, the Shah left his limousine and began the slow royal walk on the Persian carpets toward the makeshift throne. Seizing the opportunity, my trusty Bell and Howell 16mm camera was ready to record the regal event. I stepped in front of "His Majesty" and walking backward began to film. It was a great news shot... filming the face of the Shah as he walked toward me. Proudly, I was about to step aside when a gargantuan-sized bodyguard approached me to say very sternly, "Nobody walks in front of the Shah." I got the message! Apparently, I was lucky not to have been tackled by that guy. He didn't appear to have a sense of humor. So I had tea with King Constantine of Greece... and later with the Shah of Iran.

Driving along the highway, heading back to Tehran, thousands of women, fully veiled, lined the route... save one, extremely beautiful young lady who had dropped her veil. I thought at the time, 'She wants to be noticed by the Shah!'

About to experience carrier takeoffs and landings.

Chapter 10
Bribery: Guilty But Not Charged!

Arch boarding an F4 Phantom jet fighter-bomber

Now, I had what I considered to be great news film footage but it wasn't going to do me any good sitting in Iran. I had to get it back to the states for processing (it was before the wonderful days of videotaping) so I went to the airport in Tehran to post my footage off to the States. It wasn't about to be that easy.

After a lengthy discussion with a customs official, it was evident that there would be a "price" for getting the goods back to America. And we aren't talking about postage—we're talking about "greasing the palm" of the customs agent. What's a guy to do? I have this great footage (I thought) but I obviously can't get it back to the States without paying a little bribe. By the way, a "little bribe" is like being "a little bit pregnant."

So I paid the bribe and my package of film was off to the States. It's the first and only bribe I've ever paid. I did turn in that expense request to WFLA-TV for one bribe… and was reimbursed.

Somehow, my film and I finally made it back to the good 'ole United States. Mahmoud Ahmadinejad, the president (and tyrant) of Iraq would probable like the head of mine and the customs officer.

Chapter 11
That First, Lonely Leap

I read, would you believe, that skydiving in the United States had flourished to the point that it was the fastest growing sport in the nation (of course, you have to consider the base: 50 skydivers expanding to 100 is a 100 percent

Kittinger taking that long, lonely leap!

gain). Then in the early '60s, a truly daring Air Force man by the name of Captain Joseph Kittinger took to the upper atmosphere to test the effects of having to "bail out" or eject from a jet flying close to the edge of outer space.

Kittinger's jump had another purpose: to test man's ability to persevere high above the earth. Despite heavy equipment - including a 57-pound instrument pack strapped under him like a seat - he found it easy to maneuver, "All I had to do was point my left foot outward to make a right turn," he said. "To stop, I merely stuck my right foot out for a second."

Kittinger also radioed back a frightening firsthand view of space, applying equally to Americans and to the Russians. "There is a hostile sky above me," he said. "Man may live in space, but he will never conquer it."

Kittinger wrote, in his book The Long Lonely Leap:

"OVERHEAD my onion-shaped balloon spread its 200-foot diameter against a black daytime sky. More than 18 1/2 miles below lay the cloud-hidden New Mexico desert to which I shortly would parachute.

Sitting in my gondola, which gently twisted with the balloon's slow turnings, I had begun to sweat lightly, though the temperature read 36° below zero Fahrenheit. Sunlight burned in on me under the edge of an aluminized antiglare curtain and through the gondola's open door. In my earphones crackled the voice of Capt. Marvin Feldstein, one of our project's two doctors, from ground control at Holloman Air Force Base:

"Three minutes till jump, Joe." I was ready to go, for more reasons than one. For about an hour - as the balloon rose from 50,000 to 102,800 feet above sea level - I had been exposed to an environment requiring the protection of a pressure suit and helmet, and the fear of their failure had always been present. If either should break, unconsciousness would come in 10 or 12 seconds, and death within two minutes."

Captain Kittinger exited the gondola at 102,800 feet, falling 4 minutes and 35 seconds before his main chute opened (at about 13,000 feet). The temperature at that altitude was minus 94 degrees! He had exited at that altitude when he lost pressure in his right hand, which began to painfully swell. Landing in the New Mexico desert, he was quickly surrounded by medical teams from helicopters and pronounced in great shape... save the swollen right hand and a big bruise from his landing. Read his book: it is well worth it to read about one of the first pioneers of outer space!

Kittinger received the Oak Leaf cluster to the Distinguished Flying Cross. He served three combat tours in Vietnam and was a POW for 11 months. He retired in 1978 and moved to Florida, where he still enjoys flying! Kittinger was born in Tampa!

Chapter 12
The Jump Orchard

Only the dullest of people couldn't see the visual "impact" of skydiving. Actually filming a person walking into a skydive operation and hours later making his or her first jump, now that's visual, and exciting. Fortunately a nearby "orchard" for skydivers is only a short distance from Tampa. It's called Zephyrhills. Nestled about 35 miles northeast of Tampa, the little community boasts thousands of trailers, millions of egg-laying chickens, pure spring water and the name of being the most famous skydiving place in the world. What else could you want? A readymade shooting (or chuting) site with airplanes, skydivers and a chance to film a story.

The owner of the skydiving center, a character with steely blue eyes and a ready smile, stretched out his hand to welcome my crew. "I'm Jeff," said the seasoned skydiver, "we'll be glad to show you the "ropes" and teach you how easy it is to skydive. Just as easy as stepping out the door of an airplane a mile and a half above the ground," he joked. "But," he said, "you gotta watch that first step..." continuing on a roll he added, "remember when you leave the airplane, start falling."

It was obvious we'd found a Henny Youngman-type who had taking up the sport. The course consisted of several hours of instruction on what awful things your parachute could do when it fails to open properly. "The streamer," Jeff said, "doesn't slow you down, it actually speeds up your descent rate. Going feet to Earth, you create less wind resistance, therefore you get to your destination faster." The description of a horseshoe malfunction was even less appealing.

I watched as a first-jump student waddled to the aircraft wearing some old World War II (or was it WW One!?) gear with an archaic front-mount reserve. A crusty, unshaven sky-god slid over toward the already unnerved student, looked him square in the eye and in his best impersonation of Clint Eastwood muttered, "You're going to die!"

Somehow, I felt we had to improve the image of this sport a bit! Fortunately it has improved and the jump community now is a cross-section of Americana. Regularly, I jump with a psychiatrist (sure, you thought I needed a shrink) a dentist (got to smile pretty on the way down) and a host of "regular" people. Recent tests have proven it's impossible to worry about your job while skydiving! I'll second that.

Well, we're set for filming and somehow everyone is trying to talk me into making the jump! "Hey, no use using me, I've jumped before," as I tried to excuse myself. "Yeah," said Jeff, "but that airplane was going down."

We're talking about going up in a functioning aircraft. The wings are still there, it isn't on fire and you still have to jump." Well that's a different story. Try as I did, everyone thought I should be the one. 'What the heck, maybe it'll get an extra rating point or two,' I thought.

In addition to the lectures, part of the training was called the "parachute-landing fall." This is an exercise in which you see how many bruises you can put on your body in one day, jumping from a four-foot platform and slamming yourself into the ground in what should be a graceful roll. I only remembered the next day: I hurt everywhere. Even my hair hurt! But, finally, I was ready to go!

Santa goes astray

In broadcasting, or telecasting, you're only as good as your last rating book. If it goes down, you probably get the boot! Therefore, we're always trying to find ways to boost the ratings; to boost your own awareness in the community. And, after all, skydiving is a very visible sport. Many people feel you have a death wish, a notion that is absolutely the opposite of the reason people "fall into the sport.'

I began to organize: skydive into events and narrate them when I landed.

It was December and Christmas was just around the corner. What better way to get a little extra publicity (and delight the children) than to have Santa jump into a big gathering. WestShore Plaza on the west end of Tampa, coincidentally on short final approach to Tampa International Airport, was our target. The publicity folks at WestShore wanted a Santa Demo and the demonstration made for a festive occasion. Everybody, especially the kids, loved it!

To make it extra spectacular, we loaded an old 10-E Lockheed with 15 seasoned jumpers from Zephyrhills (well, at least 14 of them were seasoned). The plan was I would jump in first and narrate as a four-way team jumped, followed by a 10-person formation which, of course, included Mr. Claus.

Landing on the target, I was amazed at the huge gathering to watch a bunch of guys fall from the sky like stricken rocks. My solo jump initiated the event, allowing me a chance to fly into the target area, pick up the microphone and narrate as the remaining 14 skydivers leaped.   Shortly afterwards, the four-way team jumped from the Lockheed and landed with precision on the same tarmac target. Now it was time for the big event.

Alas, somehow the person "spotting the load" didn't do so well. We always line up the jump run upwind, so when we exit the aircraft, we use the wind to help get us back to the target, instead of fighting it. Whatever happened, the spot was bad…so bad, in fact, it was soon evident that skydivers were going to be landing all over the west end of Tampa and not with a lot of choice landing spots.   There were trees, power lines, cars and houses—lots of houses. Santa came down in a McDonald's parking lot!   That obviously delighted the kids there but didn't do much for my show.

We always have to be prepared for any circumstance so I reminded the children that Santa is more accustomed to flying a sleigh than an old Lockheed plane and skydiving was not really his thing. We sent a van to pick him up and deliver him to a cheering crowd. Everyone was just glad to see that old Saint Nick survived and there would be a Christmas after all.

At least we all survived.

Chapter 13
Celebrating a Birthday

Approaching my 40th birthday anniversary I got a "less than bright idea" to make 40 jumps in one day! Keep in mind, I only had 53 jumps at that time, but the idea was intriguing. The plan began to ferment and develop until finally, the day was at hand.

Under the Cayman Islands Parachute and 'Sir Turtle'

I was able to borrow five parachutes from friends for the attempt. Not one to relish packing the chutes, I hired a crew to pack them. Also, a golf cart was rented to run my body back to the aircraft each time, saving my energy. The Florida Citrus Commission sponsored the planned jumps, so I tossed down a gulp of OJ between each jump.

At a time like this, organization is everything! The aircraft, a Cessna 195, was outfitted for skydiving. Its original 225-horse engine had been retrofitted with a 450-hp power plant and a 3-blade propeller. The high-wing jump machine could carry 5 jumpers (legally) and the pilot.

Looking back over the jumper's logbook from that very busy day, there are notations along the way. At jump number 74, I was halfway home, tired but my spirits were high. At 12:56 I stepped out of the Cessna for the last 20 jumps. The only rest was on the plane as it climbed to altitude. On the ground I gulped more OJ and munched on a Hershey bar for energy. Somewhere along the way (the log book didn't note which jump), I experienced my first malfunction. On opening, a line wrapped over the top of my main chute; not the sort of thing you want to see. Immediately, I released the main chute, went into free fall and opened my reserve. Also steerable, the reserve put me on the target where I dropped that gear and quickly donned another to keep the pace going. The average was one jump every 9 minutes and 20 seconds. When we finally got to jump number 40, the team that had diligently packed my parachutes throughout the day wanted to go with me for the final exit. Sounded like a great idea: I just didn't know the surprise they had in store for me!

This time, we climbed not to 2500 feet, but to 9800 feet for a 45 second freefall formation. At least that's what I thought. Exiting the Cessna, we quickly put together a five-person formation. It looked and felt great, but suddenly, I was yanked out of the formation and under a rapidly opening parachute. That was part of the plan, to dump my parachute at a high altitude, as a sort of salute to the day's activities. It also put the team on the ground well ahead of me, giving them a chance to put into play the rest of their devious plan.

Finally landing on the target for my 40th jump of the day, I was all smiles until a pretty blonde (who was eventually to become my second wife, Lillian) poured champagne over my head. I really couldn't complain; it was part of the celebration. The blonde, Lillian Jackson, was a receptionist at the television station where I was anchoring the news. The evening's celebration lasted until the wee hours. I was a tired but elated newsman/skydiver.

Oh yes, to my surprise, the stunt had a great effect on the news media. The Tampa Tribune ran a full-page story with the headline: "Happy Birthday, Arch," complete with many pictures, including the one with champagne running over my head. Apparently, you could call this a successful publicity stunt. That was not the original intent, but that's the way it ended. Imagine parachute gear, soaked in champagne and left in a hot trunk for a day. Ugh! You can only imagine the stench of stale, overheated champagne!

My television opponent on the "other" channel, the late Hugh Smith of Channel 13 News, mused, "I guess I'll have to get a job packing parachutes." Little did either of us know before long I would be the subject of a major news story and he would be interviewing me.

I merely mentioned that "little blonde" who doused me with champagne: there are more details. Constantly traveling on news assignments and working long hours at the television station, my marriage was not getting the

Skydiving over Grand Cayman, BWI

time it needed and deserved. If any blame could be placed, I would have to accept it. As I said, I'm getting smarter each year.

The 50 jumps in one day (an average of leaving the airplane every 6 minutes and 20 seconds), I felt, was somewhat of an accomplishment. However, in 2007, a former member of the U.S. Army's Golden Knights, Jay Stokes performed 642 jumps in one 24-hour period. When he finished he admitted, "I'm a little tired." What an accomplishment. Jay, your record is safe; I will never challenge it!

As the ratings for my station soared, the management wanted me to do the major news shows at 6 and 11pm, seven days a week. The newspaper ads blurted: "The Best Deal at 6 and 11pm," and it worked. That stint lasted four years, and the marriage suffered further. But, I allowed myself to be used in this manner. With four children, whom I loved and still love dearly, Margaret and I divorced each other (but not the children). Later, I began to wonder what happened, like a lady who just had a baby and is encountering postpartum depression; I guess that would best describe my dilemma. Darn, hindsight is always so perfect!

Lillian ("that pretty, little blonde") got involved in real estate and later with mortgage banking; and I got "involved" with her! She was exceptionally skillful in her field. I inherited a stepdaughter, Sheila, who was a handful as a teenager. However, she grew up to be a beautiful lady with a matching personality. She wound up in the Cayman Islands married to a successful developer.

Lillian's father was born in the Caymans and that gave me the chance to make the first jump into Cayman Brac (one of three islands that comprise the Caymans).

Linten Tibbets, owner of Cox Lumber, had purchased an airline, albeit rather small. "Red Carpet" it was called, and its mission was to fly from Tampa to the Cayman Islands. It was an adventurous undertaking that lasted for a while. It also gave me the chance to perform in the Caymans. Tibbets arranged the event, and we were off, bound for those beautiful islands south of Cuba.

Imagine being on a lush tropical island where no one had ever seen a sky dive (except on television)! Students were released from school on the auspicious day to watch people jump from a "perfectly good airplane." As I also have said, there is no such thing as a "perfectly good" airplane. If there's dirt on the floor or a scratch in the paint it isn't perfect!

The jump came off before a delighted group of children who stood in awe watching us repack our chutes. Our host took us on a tour of the island, which includes the Bluffs! The promontories reach high above the Caribbean, with caves that provided protection from hurricanes over the years. Cayman Brac is well known for its spectacular wall diving, but lately it is also developing a reputation for some of the world's most exotic rock climbing. The 140-foot bluffs of the island provide dramatic vistas and challenging climbs. A number of world-renowned climbers have built homes on the Brac. Two such people are Liz Grenard and John Byrnes.

My sport (skydiving) is far less strenuous. In fact, we let gravity do all the work!

Page 52

After the guided tour, it was off to Grand Cayman and a Lions Club celebration. We were to perform in an area south of North Sound on an undeveloped tract. Our host for that performance was a native Caymanian with a very familiar Cayman name: Atlee Bodden. Atlee asked a question I couldn't answer, "What should we charge for admission to a skydiving show in the Caymans?" Well, we had performed at many air shows but we were

On Seven-Mile Beach, Grand Cayman ... team member Chris Mangos gathering my 'chute.

always a "portion" of the entertainment. There were always many acrobatic aircraft and war birds. In this case, "we" were the show: the only show.

When the time came to jump, we used a DC-3 passenger plane. Along for the ride was the British-appointed governor of the island. We strapped him and other guests facing back so they could watch the exit from the plane, affectionately called a "Gooney Bird." As we prepared to jump, we could see a long line of auto traffic from Georgetown, the main city, to the jump site. "Wait!" I commanded. "Let's wait for the rest of the spectators to arrive and then we'll jump." It proved to be a successful event for the Lions Club and we made several jumps that day, savoring the gorgeous view of the Islands and the Caribbean from two miles up.

In the following years, we made many trips to that beautiful island and often did skydiving performances. The Cayman Islands government sponsored International Aviation Week every year in June and each year we performed several shows for the Cayman people, first jumping on Seven Mile Beach, then rushing to repack and get back into the sky for a jump into the airport. Everyone heads for the airport to view the aircraft, including military jets, up close and personal.

The next day, we were up early in the Caribbean sunshine to fly to Cayman Brac. The Brac people loved the skydive exhibitions. In fact, many of them, octogenarians, had never been off that "rock." As we landed on the tarmac of the Brac airport, many looked at us as if we were gods! We found a cooler place to repack in the baggage department and later boarded the aircraft for the 90-minute flight back to the mainland of Grand Cayman. Those weeks in the June sun of Grand Cayman were the very best. Great fun, super skydives and wonderful people.

At one of the shows, we gave them more of a show than we had intended. Performing for Miller Brewing Company all over America, we had 80 different parachutes covering the three brands for which we performed: Miller Lite, Miller Genuine Draft and Miller High Life. That many parachutes always brings up Murphy's Law: Anything that can go wrong will and at the worst possible time.

On the way to the airport I wondered to myself, 'who packed this parachute? Should I repack it?' 'Naw! It'll be fine,' I mused. I should have known better.

In the sky over the Caribbean, our team exited at 10,500 feet above the island to perform our "Six Pack in the Sky," a beautiful formation of six canopies stacked one over the other. After opening shock, you first look up to check your canopy to make sure it's opened properly.

Looking up I got a shock: The lettering on the parachute was backward, meaning only one thing; the parachute was on backwards. Decision time! First, part of your training is that you never cut away (breakaway or jettison) a good parachute. It's backward, and flying that way, but it's still a good parachute! The only difference, besides flying backwards at about 20 miles per hour, is that the steering is reversed. Pull down on the right steering toggle and you get a right turn? Nope, you get a left turn. Conversely, pulling the left toggle rewards you with a right turn. You have to keep your head very clear and think carefully before controlling the chute.

The first inclination (and a good one) is to find a clear spot inland to place the landing. However, as I got lower and lower, I got the weird idea that I could land that chute on the beach, near the target, all the time flying backwards. The approach to the target was over power lines on the highway and tall Australian Pines, then the beach and beyond that lots of blue water, more than you ever wanted to see.

Deep water, too! In fact the Cayman Trench is the second deepest spot in the ocean, second only to the Marianas Trench off the Philippines.

Decision time, flying backwards over the water, I thought carefully and quickly and initiated a turn back toward the beach. Now I was really moving. Below me was the beautiful water; behind me, the beach where I dearly wanted to land.

Looking down, I watched the water beneath my feet. As soon as I saw sand, I quickly flared the parachute, bringing down both steering lines simultaneously to stop the speed and hopefully give me a soft landing.

The target I made; the landing…well, I was happy I wore a helmet. It was heels, butt and head as I slammed into the white, but very hard sand. I saw stars, but I made it, and there were no after effects with the exception of always being kidded in the Islands by the air show crew who wanted to know when I planned another "backward landing." I assured them that the idea was just "too much show." I've been there, done that!

That's me, lower left, and then clockwise, Charlie Hammond, Annemarie Gueli Hammond and Dr. Steven Groff.

Chapter 14
Back to Cypress Gardens

Now, let's get back to that eventful day at Cypress Gardens.

You'll always know when it's summertime in Florida. The humidity is a dead giveaway. I wouldn't trade it for anywhere else, but it does get hot and sticky that time of year. We kid that we have all kinds of weather in Florida - we just don't have any that make us have to shovel!

Cypress Gardens, Florida from the sky,

This particular time of year was being noted at Cypress Gardens, Florida - a Florida Icon: the home of water skiing and ante-bellum costumes, once the major tourist attraction in Florida, until Mickey and SeaWorld moved in! The annual Summer Festival was to be June 21 and 22nd. To note this auspicious occasion, my team of professional skydivers was invited to perform for the event, promoted conspicuously on my television station. "Come out for the Cypress Gardens Summer Festival, where anchorman Arch Deal will skydive in and sign autographs." Pretty hokey, but we do things like that in radio and television to get ratings.

We had arranged for a 4-pack jump - three others and me. Generally, I would dive out of the Cessna 182 first, land on the target, pick up the microphone and narrate the rest of the show as my compatriots would dive out at 7,500 feet and fall one mile in 30 seconds while holding hands.

It was hot and sticky along Lake Eloise (where the water skiers perform) when we arrived in Cypress Gardens on Friday evening, prior to the Festival. As skydivers are known to do, we partied late and well into that evening, looking forward to a great weekend in the sky and on the ground.

On Saturday morning, the tourists began to pile into the Gardens. Shortly, they were as thick as the humidity and swarming like the honeybees around the Gardens' flowers.

It was an ideal day for our shows, with cumulus clouds just beginning to build, a long way off from producing the typical Florida Summer afternoon showers.

The day went well, with no hitches. Our Cessna 182, Flown by ace aviator Bud Clark of Lakeland, arrived on time at the tiny Cypress Gardens grass landing field. Paul Latham, airport manager and owner of Cypress Gardens Aviation, greeted us as we unpacked our gear from the van and prepared for each jump. In later years, I was to add a wireless microphone so I could narrate each show from the sky as we performed our aerial maneuvers. But, for now, I had to be satisfied with performing a solo jump, land by the microphone and then narrate the remainder of the show as the other three jumpers performed for the crowd. It was a show idea that seemed to work very well and that first day of the summer of '75 it was a hit!

June 22nd dawned a carbon copy Florida summer day. Hot, humid, but darned beautiful. It was going to be a dynamite day for our performances. The television station, WFLA-TV, paid to have the parachute lettered and promoted the event throughout the week. The campaign worked: The place was crawling with tourists.

Prior to heading for the airplane, we walked on the grass in front of the grandstand viewing area between the crowds and the water ski show to check out our landing area. It looked great! It was inviting for a skydiving show before a full house. As we made our way back to the van, I spotted Red McGuire, chief photographer for the Gardens. "Hey Red," I yelled across the grass, "make sure you get some good shots of our parachutes and our spectacular landings here!" "Sure, will," Red quipped, "I'll have my eye to the sky and ready to shoot the chutes."

Later, that was going to be a big disappointment for Red. He was just about to miss the major picture opportunity of his career. If it had occurred in this decade, hundreds of mini-cams and cell phones would be recording the skydive.

We jumped into the van and drove to the little Cypress Gardens airport, where we unloaded our gear into the office of airport manager Paul Latham. We used the buddy system every time we jump. It's a system whereby everybody checks everybody else's gear. It's easy to spot a potential problem that way. A twisted leg strap may feel right but it can lead to a towed pilot chute, which gets you to the ground much too fast. Everything checked out, and we were finally ready to go.

Having been on thousands of jumps, I found you always have to "back-time" to allow for any unexpected exigency that may occur. Basically, we always had to be on time, much the same as being on time for your broadcast or telecast. There can be no excuses!

The Cessna, flown by Bud Clark, roared to life as we climbed aboard. It was the standard jump plane for small drop zones. It was capable of carrying four jumpers and the pilot to altitude in scant minutes.

Bud jockeyed the plane into position and, after a magneto check, the throttle was pushed to the maximum. We began to roll down the grass strip. There are advantages to grass strips: They're easier on your tires. The disadvantages include a longer takeoff roll and a short field takeoff procedure. No hitch, everything purred along as the pilot rotated the Cessna and easily cleared the power lines that like to haunt every small strip.

Climbing over the Gardens was a beautiful sight. There are actually five lakes that surround the scenic spot, all ringed by majestic cypress trees. The main one, in front of the crowd, is Lake Eloise. As we passed overhead, looking out the right side of the aircraft where the door had been removed for our jump, we could see the huge crowd assembled for our show. A few were there to watch the water skiers! I say that in jest, because their performers were second to none. Every time I watched them, I knew I had the easy job.

Page 59

They were superb professionals. As a person who lived on a bay in Tampa, I had two boats: one for fun and fishing, the other for cruising and water skiing. Along with the family, we spent most weekends letting the younger Deals gain their proficiency on the skis, either standard, slalom or banana skis. It was great fun for the entire family and me. My daughter, Karen, became very proficient on the single ski and daughter Diane was always eager to ski over Tampa Bay.

Getting ready for this jump reminded me of the time I performed a charity benefit sky dive in Sun City, Florida. I was delighted to meet at that show a gentleman who received and deserved the admiration of circus fans everywhere. The Great Karl Wallenda was the major attraction. He was walking the tight wire for a huge group of children.

It was an outstanding honor to meet this gentleman and I told him so as we shook hands. "Arch," he said, "I could never do what you do." I was astounded! I certainly could never do what he did with such eloquence. After all, in sky diving, gravity does most of the work. Gravity and our parachutes are our friends. We couldn't perform without either one. We remembered the comment from the 1920s that stated, "of 20,000 feet of fall, remember, it's the last half inch that hurts." I was about to experience the truth in that axiom. Despite being involved in several tragedies in his family's acts, Karl, a native of Germany, continued with his death-defying stunts. In 1978, at age 73, Karl attempted a walk between the two towers of the ten-story Condado Plaza Hotel in San Juan, Puerto Rico, on a wire stretched 121 feet above the pavement, but fell to his death when winds exceeded 30 miles per hour. The Wallenda family attributes the tragedy to misconnected guide ropes along the wire and not the windy conditions. A year later, Karl's eldest grandson, Rick Wallenda went back and completed the walk successfully.

Meanwhile, back in the Cessna jump plane, we dropped our yellow wind streamers at about 2,000 feet above the target. They are crepe paper weighted devices that give us a wind indication well above the target. Today, the wind was out of the southeast, putting our exit point about a mile and a half southeast of the Gardens, over an old mature, unused citrus grove.

JUMP RUN

At 1:39 pm, we turned jump run from over Lake Eloise, heading into the wind, like more than a thousand times before. I would not describe this as "old hat" or boring. In fact, if it weren't exciting, I wouldn't be doing it.

Looking out of the aircraft, it appeared this course would take us over our target. Time now: 1:41 and we're over the target and continuing on our heading. I shout corrections to Pilot Clark, "five right!" and he skids the plane another five degrees to make that minute correction. Another five right, and the Cessna is coming up right over the spot. "You guys have a great, safe jump!" I shouted to my colleagues in the back of the airplane. To Pilot Clark I yelled "thanks for the ride, see you below!" (as Jacques Cousteau would say.)

1:42pm, I'm out the door and in free fall. Perhaps we call it "free fall" because the fall doesn't cost anything. You pay for the ride in the airplane to altitude. Amazingly there is no feeling of falling. When you leave, your body is going the same speed as the plane. Without a propeller on your nose and no aluminum skin, your forward speed begins to diminish as your sink rate increases. Therefore, your body is "flying" all the time. That is difficult for most to understand: they just look at you incredulously! Something magical happens after you have accelerated for about 12 seconds. You have reached "terminal velocity." Sounds scary doesn't it? Actually it only means your body is falling as fast as it's going to fall in a given position. Pull in your arms or legs and you accelerate. Dive head down and you can come close to 200 miles per hour.

But all the while you feel like you're floating on the world's biggest air mattress, being supported by this column of air. This happens because the air resistance of your body finally balances the pull of gravity. It helps to remind yourself that in the flat and stable position, you're still getting closer to the ground by one thousand feet every five seconds.

The Cessna and I parted company at 3,000 feet above the ground. I would reach terminal and come in for the pull to be open at 2,000 feet above the old grapefruit grove. That's the altitude at which basic safety rules say we must be open. It's only a rule, but disobey it and it will catch up with you. Skydiving, like flying, is basically a safe sport. But both are unforgiving of carelessness. A crusty skydiver was heard to cite the eleventh commandment, "Forget to pull and the ground shall smite thee!"

Quickly, the seconds and the altitude tick away. 2,500 feet by the altimeter, and in another 2.5 seconds I'm approaching two thousand feet. As I have 743 times before, I came in quickly and smoothly for the pull. Most skydivers wear a "ground alert," an altimeter mounted on the back of the hand or chest strap that shows how high they are from the ground (or impact). The day before I joked with the crowd at the Gardens about the altimeter. "When

Mickey's hand gets to the Red, it's time to pull." A common yarn I spin is, "When people look like ants, PULL. When ants look like people, why bother!"

As the ripcord is yanked I anticipate the smooth tug of the deployment of the chute. But there is nothing! Where is that friendly embracing yank that indicates the parachute is opening!? Looking over my shoulder, I see the pilot chute bouncing around in the dead-air space over my back: a pilot chute hesitation. No big worry! You just try to look over your shoulder. That'll twist your body enough to allow air to flow over and carry the pilot chute away. Sounds simple enough, but for some reason it didn't happen. Instead, the pilot chute was dancing madly across the bag that holds the main parachute when suddenly the bag starts to lift off my back with the pilot chute wrapped around it. Not a pretty sight. In fact, it is a very ugly sight! I realize I have a "bag-lock!" The parachute isn't about to open. It can't! It has been sealed shut by the bridle of the pilot chute. Now I know it's time to take rapid action. The response called for is "Reserve deployment," and fast. It's bad enough to have a malfunction where your chute can't open; in this case, the drag of the pilot chute and bag, with lines fluttering in the wind is just enough to draw your body feet to earth and increase your descent speed to about 150 mph. You begin to realize this is not your best day!

Thinking back on the day, I remembered that old salty skydiver who was instructing a student on reserve deployment. He said, "With this front-mounted reserve chute, you bring your knees up, uncover the devices that release the parachute from the harness. This jettisons the malfunction so you can then open the reserve in clean air." "What," asked the student, "do you do if the reserve doesn't open?" "Well," replied the instructor, "you twist your legs together!" "What good does that do?" the worried student queried. "None at all," said the instructor. "It just makes it easier to screw you out of the ground."

Following that prudent advice, I raised my knees, uncovered the releases and hammered down sharply on both sides. Prior to this, my reserve had been called into play on a couple of other occasions, and the system worked fine. Each time, there was a smooth response and the reserve landed me safely. However, this was not to be!

As I yanked down on the releases, only the right side let go, putting greater, unequal pressure on the left side, which then steadfastly refused to budge.

No time to squander. I'm now under one thousand feet with impact in less than 4 seconds. I grab the reserve across the middle, yank the ripcord, tossing it to the citrus grove and throw the reserve outward in an effort to get it to miss the tangled lines and open beside the bag-locked main chute. I hurl as vigorously as I can with the extra adrenaline pumping through my body. The white reserve chute, a military 24-foot model, caught in the fierce 150 mph wind stream went up and wrapped around the lines of the hapless main chute.

'There goes my whole day,' I thought! My future looked very grim indeed. Over the years, the common question from those who asked me about this fall is, "What was on your mind on the way down?" Well, besides fast (very fast) prayers, I thought, 'If I don't get this parachute open, I'm going to die. No one can hit the ground at over 120 miles per hour and survive.' The second item on my mind? 'How much is that going to hurt?'

Back at the airfield, Paul Latham is watching from the ground. He was later to tell reporters, "As the chute opened, I noticed right away it was a streamer because it didn't balloon. It didn't open, in other words. I waited a few seconds and I could see Arch reaching for something on his right shoulder and then all of a sudden it went away, wherever the strings were. When they left, the other side didn't release at all and he reached down and I could see his hands come down and pull the reserve chute that was in front of him. But it just started up and it just started wrapping around, and then I ran into the office and called for an ambulance."

Latham, who wore a chute in World War Two and dropped other jumpers, watched the scene unfold with binoculars. He said neither parachute took any air whatsoever. He didn't see the impact but once it was obvious, he ran for the phone. He did say I looked awfully busy up there on the way down.

Talk about busy; man, was I ever! Looking up into what might appear to be a hopeless mess, you just can't give up and kick and scream until impact. I yanked and pulled on the lines, trying and trying to get something to catch air, thinking maybe tonight we'll sit at dinner and I'll tell the guys, "You won't believe how close I was when the chute finally opened." It would make a great "there I was" story.

But it was grim; with what would appear to be scant seconds or milliseconds left, I glanced over my shoulder to see the ground coming to meet me. In skydiving even from 15,000 feet to 2,500 feet, the ground never rushes to meet you.... unless you're too close. Then it comes at you (believe me) like a freight train expanding in size as it approaches.

IMPACT!

Suddenly the ground and were one! No more free fall, no more fighting with the tangled, flailing lines of the unopened chutes. That part of the skydive was over. Now there was pain, excruciating, flashing pain throughout my body. The impact, which must have been close to 120 miles per hour, sent my body into the old abandoned grapefruit field, right beside a mature grapefruit tree.

But, wait a minute; I feel pain, I see light! What's happening here? This cannot be. You can't possibly have survived that impact, so there shouldn't be any pain or light. Just as suddenly, the light went away, not because of a loss of consciousness, but from the dust, dirt and debris unearthed when I crashed into the soft, sandy soil of the citrus grove. It all fell back into my face, blinding me, but only for a while.

Then, with the pain, there was silence. There was peacefulness no one else could ever know unless they're in same or similar position. While there was no illumination from the Florida sun on that hot, second day of summer in that old field, there was another brilliant and pure light that transcended everything else. I had spent my entire life as a television news reporter, assessing, analyzing the facts and describing them to the viewers. Now, I was without words to describe my feelings. Even today, I cannot express the serenity and peace an individual, albeit broken up, can feel, alone. Just me and my thoughts were lying in that old weed-strewn field. But it was a peace beyond belief!

Over the years I have never forgotten the overwhelming feeling in that immaculate light. There was no pain, just an inner comfort that I could never begin to describe. Perhaps there are other things for me to do! God decided it was not my time, that perhaps he wasn't ready for me, or that I have much more to do!

But now, that light was beginning to fade. Inexorably, the pain began to reassert itself and as that pure white light began to extinguish, the realization returned: that I was alone, lying broken, beside an old citrus tree I couldn't see. How long I laid there, I later found out, was not an eternity, but well over a half hour. The Tampa Tribune report said the impact left my body

18 inches into the ground. Sounds a little far-fetched, however I didn't take the time to get up and measure! Nah! Maybe six to eight, but not eighteen. Come on!

I began to contemplate over the events of a lifetime. Among those thoughts was how I came to be in this place. It started with broadcasting, and wound up in a citrus grove.

A Spectator's Viewpoint

This was written by a spectator who witnessed the event:

In 1975, after breakfast on a Sunday morning in June, as was our custom, the question before us was, "Where shall we fly to today?" Our children, then ages nine, seven and five (two boys, a girl), voted to go for a picnic at Cypress Gardens. Our Lake Amphibian was anchored at our home on Lake Tarpon for the weekend. All was promptly made ready and forty minutes later we landed, water-taxied up, and were setting anchor at Cypress Gardens in Winter Haven. We chose our usual safe spot from where we could swim, picnic and watch the famous Cypress Garden Water Ski Show.

Sometime after lunch, while swimming with the kids, Steve happened to be facing east and caught sight of what he described as an "incredible scene" in the distant sky far above our heads. What he observed was a partially inflated parachute about a mile or so away, descending rather rapidly towards the earth! A skydiver himself, as he reported this, he was completely aware of the unhappiness related to this circumstance and he kept hoping, as he followed the chute's downward path, that it would either blossom fully open or be cutaway and replaced with something more pleasing to the eye. He followed it down as it disappeared behind the tree line, and neither of the above had occurred! So, he scooped everyone up into the amphibian and immediately flew over to the Lake Wales Airport, which was on the southern border adjacent to the lake. There a car was borrowed, and he drove over to where he estimated the event had occurred. Upon arrival at the site, those there informed him that indeed an accident occurred. The jumper was doing a "Demo Jump" (a demonstration made for some festive occasion) and experienced a partial malfunction during the deployment of his parachute.

The fall was luckily broken somewhat by his coming down on a tree. "Who was it?" "It was Arch Deal. The ambulance just took him away, and they're bringing him to the St. Joseph's Hospital in Tampa!" Now Steve was beside himself. He not only knew Arch but also had jumped with him only the week before at the Skydiving Center in Zephyrhills. Steve brought the car back to Lake Wales where we were all waiting and again loaded us up in the amphibian. We then flew to Tampa International Airport. From there, the family was sent home and Steve got a lift over to St. Joseph's Hospital. As Steve was on the Medical Staff there, despite orders for anonymity due to Arch's celebrity, he found out where they had taken him and went directly there. Expecting the worst, he entered the room.

There was Arch! Lying flat on his back, arms up with hands clasped behind his head......and Smiling! Smiling!! "Hi, Steve." "Hi, Arch." After some amazed minutes of pleasant conversation, Steve left. It was then, he says, that he began to feel how shaken inside he really was. Downstairs on the way out of the hospital he came upon the EMS people who brought Arch in. They somewhat incredulously reported that from the moment they picked him up (literally), he never lost consciousness, and never complained. For the most part, he told jokes and just had a smile on his face. After all, he was a Television News Anchor and was just doing his job (I guess).

Since then, Arch and Steve have made many more jumps together, the most recent being Sunday, August 31st; that's 28 years post Big Bounce. And yes, there are more unusual Arch Deal experiences that can be told, but that perhaps is for another story.

In the annals of skydiving, there have been other miraculous escapes from death even after striking the ground at close to 100 miles per hour.

A member of the Army's Golden Knights had such an encounter when his malfunctioning parachutes had him impacting in the newly-sodded lawn of a doctor's home. The physician raced out to aid the skydiver until the emergency crews arrived. I always wondered if he charged for a house call!!!!

The injured knight, after a lengthy stay in the hospital and recuperation, did return to the sky to jump again.

Another even more frightful event occurred in the sky over Yuma, Arizona, where the elite Golden Knights practiced their exciting skills. One of the most thrilling was the "Diamond track" in which two performers would exit the aircraft at 12,500 feet and simultaneously track (glide) away from each other. Red smoke grenades, connected to the boots of each performer, trailed across the sky like contrails showing the path of speed of each jumper. They would gain speeds of 150 miles per hour. Then they would fly back toward each other to cross each other's path, forming a diamond in the sky. This day, Sgt. First Class Dana Bowman was performing with Sgt. Jose Aguillon. This, however was to be a disastrous day for both of them. Between 4,500 and 3,500 feet their closing speed was close to 300 miles per hour. In a split second, they realized they were too close! They collided at about 300 miles per hour. Knocked unconscious, Dana hit the pavement of a parking lot with a partially deployed chute. Jose was in freefall when an automatic opener deployed his chute at about 750 feet. However, it wasn't enough to save his life. He died six hours later.

Dana was unconscious for two days. The fellow knights were around when he awoke. They had to tell him that Jose, his friend had died. Dana had lost both of his legs in the collision.

He was about to be discharged from the Army, but with sheer determination he was not about to leave. Staying at the Army's Walter Reed Hospital, Dana returned to Fort Bragg, North Carolina. With his colleagues, he made his first jump since the horrendous accident. Nine months after the terrible impact, Dana became the first double amputee to ever re-enlist in the U.S. Army. After 18 years, he did retire, but continued to snow ski, water ski, scuba dive and make over 500 parachute jumps after his accident. He became the world's first double-amputee helicopter instructor. Whatta man!

Over the years, I have had many occasions to jump on the same venue with the Golden Knights and also when they would visit our favorite drop zones. They are a super tribute to the men and women of our military.

Chapter 16
No Stranger to Malfunctions

The word "malfunction" is never an expression a skydiver wants to hear. We were trained early that this sort of thing could occur and you must be prepared to deal with it. After all, hurtling toward the ground at 120 miles per hour is no time to think to yourself, 'Darn, now what am I supposed to do?' You could spend the rest of your life (10 seconds) thinking about it!

After I transitioned from the old round cheapo parachutes to the ultra modern "squares," the term became more of a reality. A dropzone regular asked, as I strapped on my rig, "how many mals (malfunctions) have you had?" "None," I confidently replied, "I think a malfunction is a state of mind," I added, all too smugly! "Well," he added, "you're going to have some now."

He implied the modern rectangular chute was more prone to malfunction. That just isn't true. Today, the chute is far safer than the old round ones. However, during the initial testing of the new type gliding device, problems did occur. These were caused principally by the deployment systems used to open the chutes without jarring your body to a state of unconsciousness. Initially, a myriad of ideas were tried and "canned" for something else. You see, without some sort of "reefing system," the rectangular chute would open so fast and so hard you wouldn't want to think about it.

It was in the days of experimentation for squares. Eventually, someone thought of the simplest and safest device. It came to be known as a "slider" because it would slide down the parachute lines as it opened, providing a smoother and much more enjoyable experience. Until that time, malfunctions were many! Earlier, I mentioned that I was no stranger to a tangled parachute. Testing this new flying device made me "air out" my reserve several times before Cypress Gardens, and three times after. Trying out new ideas has its price.

One such day came over Zephyrhills, the Central Florida "jumper orchard." The "Ten High Bunch" was carrying out its regular weekend practice sessions, looking ahead to the fall and the November Turkey Meet. I was "base" man for the bunch, an assortment of individuals who just loved to be in the sky and who wanted to be the fastest group to form a 10-person circle in the sky.

Being base meant I was first out the door of the crowded Lockheed 10E (the sort in which Amelia Earhart vanished). The other nine would dive after me and form a circle as rapidly as possible. We felt on top of the world when we could do that in less than 12 seconds. Today, in competition, that's dreadfully slow.

That particular day I was trying out a new rig, a new type of parachute container that promised to be more compact. It also featured a new routing of the ripcord to protect it from being accidentally activated. It worked, only too well!

Completing our maneuvers, we broke at 3,500 feet, each person turning 180 degrees from the center and tracking (or gliding) away from each other. Five seconds later, with a wave of my hands to signal any nearby jumpers, I pulled the ripcord. Then, pulled it again and again and again: the darn thing wouldn't come out! Something awful went wrong; the ripcord could not be extracted.

With both hands, I yanked with all the adrenaline my body (now in a head-down position and accelerating) could muster. 'No use,' I thought. 'It's not coming out.' Below my chin, fastened to my chest, however, was a nice flat reserve parachute with a bright, shiny handle. Without wasting further time, I extracted the reserve's handle and received instant response.

In a flash, the bundle of white nylon was yanked from the reserve container and exploded into action. My downward descent was probably close to 150 mph due to using both hands in trying to pull the ripcord. At least I had a parachute; or did I? Looking up, after the spine-wrenching opening, I didn't see the pretty sight I had expected. Five lines of the parachute had been ripped away, and there were numerous panels in the chute blown away. In fact, I believe you could have driven a Volkswagen through one of the big holes. This did not look good!

Above, my teammates saw my struggle and the very low opening. They couldn't see the holes but they could see that the parachute, or what remained of it, had a mind of its own. It was flying itself, sort of like a paper airplane. It turned one way, then the other diving once toward the runway and then turning toward a sagebrush field. I was coming out of the sky as if I were being ejected from it. This, I thought, is going to have to be one of the best parachute landing falls anywhere to minimize bone breakage.

Suddenly, at a high descent rate but also with a high forward speed, I smacked into the field and "bounced" (the teammates told me) two or three times. Then, I just laid there. "Damn, that hurt," I thought out loud. I tried to move and found, to my amazement, everything was intact; nothing was broken! "Wow," I yelled as I jumped up, "that was a heck of a ride." I could never have imagined that, in the future, I would have one without benefit of either parachute.

Back at the parachute loft, we tried to simulate the freefall position and tried again to extract the recalcitrant ripcord. No luck, it would not come out. "Oh, well," I said, "it's back to the drawing board for this rig." I ditched it and never used it again.

Meanwhile, back at the airport, and at the Gardens, a mild sort of chaos was underway. George Prescott, the Gardens' announcer was first telling the crowd, "well folks, Arch Deal opened his chute back behind us and will be flying around to land shortly." Later, he amended that to say the show had been canceled for the day. With that, the crowds began to mill about, wondering what, if anything had gone wrong. Perhaps some wanted their money back.

My little jump team was back on the field. Having watched me "go in" they did not jump but decided to land and help in the search for the body. Rushing to exit the field as quickly as possible, one jammed the key in the ignition upside down and broke it off. Still, the vehicle started and the three rushed toward that old citrus field. At the same time, an ambulance was on its way from Winter Haven. It wasn't rushing at all!

They had been told that a parachutist went into the ground without a parachute! So, why risk someone else's life in an effort to retrieve a dead body?

I couldn't argue with that logic. Besides, I had nowhere to go. I was just lying around, assembling my thoughts in my broken body. Obviously, I wouldn't be dancing tonight!

What had broken in that sudden meeting between my body and terra firma? As the pain increased, I knew I couldn't move at all. However, I felt I could wiggle my fingers and my toes! What a relief! Somehow I knew I would survive this thing and be whole again. Pain was a sort of blessing at that point. I could deal with it because to me it meant two things. First, that I was alive and second, that I wasn't paralyzed. Later, I was to find the extent of my injuries; a bilateral ring fracture of the second cervical vertebrae, one millimeter from being a classic "hangman's break." Six ribs were broken, but that only hurt when I laughed. You really don't want to start coughing with broken ribs. Lumbar vertebrae one and two were crushed together. Later I would tell everyone I used to be six inches taller. Actually, the two vertebrae fused together, making my navel an inch closer to my Adam's apple. The pelvis was separated, and my legs were broken. Oh, yes, besides a lot of internal stuff, I also had a scratch on my nose! One of the ace Gardens skiers had loaned me his helmet fitted with a hydraulic padding. It bounced away on impact, probably adding the nose scratch on the way. However, it may have provided the additional padding that prevented a fractured skull!

Searching through the undergrowth of the old citrus grove, my team members couldn't find me anywhere. One of the jumpers, who said he knew I was dead, suddenly shouted out in frustration, "Arch, where are you?" "Over here," I replied in as strong a voice as I could muster. He said he almost had a cardiac at that point. They ran in the direction of the response but stopped about 15 feet short. "You go ahead. We'll wait here," one said to the others. "I'm okay." I said with confidence that certainly belied my condition.

The jumpers, Donald 'Ski' Chmielewski, his wife Donna, Pat Moore and his wife Connie were over me.

Then, I could hear the pain in their voices as they asked, "what can we do for you, Arch?" "Get the dirt out of my eyes, so I can see," was my most ardent request. Carefully, they removed the sand and dust from my eyes and the light returned. And with it, one of the grimmest sights you can imagine. I looked up to see three very somber individuals. Obviously, they needed some cheering up. So, I started joking with them while we waited for the ambulance attendants to arrive.

Tongue in cheek, I chastised them for not "going on with the show" after my malfunction. It was good to have them by me. Just how good I was about to find out.

The ambulance finally found the spot and the two attendants were by me seconds later. What happened then was rather amazing. "Let's drag him out into a clearing so we can put him on a stretcher." commanded one to the other. "Whoa, wait a moment," ordered one of my teammates! "Don't you guys have an orthopedic scoop?" "An ortha-what?" the first attendant queried. "Never mind," my guys said, "wait here, we'll get it out of the ambulance." My teammates went to the ambulance, found the orthopedic scoop and rapidly returned. This device, in two sections, enables helpers to place one piece on each side of the body and scoop under the body, finally joining in the middle.   It makes it possible to "scoop up" a body with the minimum of movement.

Imagine me with a neck fractured within one millimeter of a classic hangman's break, being dragged into the clearing. A good sneeze could have done me in. Fortunately, there was no ragweed blowing about and I didn't have a cold. Apparently, I am one of the lucky ones again: I don't catch colds... well, maybe once every twelve years or so, and it's gone in two days or less!

Chapter 17
On The Road Again

As the ambulance did its wheelie into the Winter Haven Hospital emergency room entrance area, the doctors were probably preparing for the autopsy. At least that's what they said later. I absolutely looked terrible when they wheeled the stretcher out of the ambulance. Hair mussed and all. To my wife—Lillian at the time-who had expected to be a widow, I simply added, "Stick around; we'll go dancing." It seemed the appropriate thing to say at that time. Everybody looked so grim!

Also, much later, I was to learn the doctors said I shouldn't be alive and couldn't possibly last through the night. Now wait a cotton-picking minute! I didn't bounce in that citrus grove to die in a hospital although hospitals can be dangerous; they're full of sick people, and there are lots of diseases around. You have to be careful!

Everything was STAT from there on, except for me. I was being administered glucose and blood to replace that lost in the internal bleeding. Into those plastic tubes the doctors and nurses slipped some mighty powerful drugs. Until that time, I was totally cognizant of everything about me.

Now, suddenly, I was slipping off into Nah-Nah land, without a worry in the world. I was back up in the sky, floating around on Cloud Number Nine to Twenty and I didn't need a parachute. It wasn't the kind of flying I wanted to do. The pure fresh air in your hair and your "knees in the breeze" is all the stimulus you ever need.

I reflected on my first and only experience with those who may have used drugs or somehow got in trouble with the law, when I later was to put on a demonstration jump for a bunch of juvenile offenders in a Florida corrections facility. After jumping in, I told the younger group of "shut-ins" that there was a much better, ultimate "high." It's not illegal, immoral or fattening, and it's a heck of a lot safer. We call it "free fall." We did cause a bit of a problem for the warden at the prison; even though he approved the jump, he never realized (until later) that he would have four more bodies checking out of the compound than had checked in! That's the way you determine if someone is missing. It took a little balancing of the books for that one.

Through the night, the medical staff played with my broken bones while cardiologists and neurologists studied my condition. With that, they upgraded my condition to perhaps being able to last two nights instead of one.

Day two, among the splints and bandages, I managed somehow to get my hands on a telephone that someone carelessly left nearby. I've always said, "You can always tell an old anchorman: you just can't tell them much."

I dialed Cypress Gardens and asked for Pat Callahan, who was the Public Relations Director at that time. He quickly answered. "Pat," I squeaked, "this is Arch Deal." "This must be your idea of a sick joke!" Pat angrily snarled. "Arch Deal is in critical condition at the hospital, and I don't think you're very funny!" "But, Pat," I pleaded, "This is Arch. Somebody left a phone nearby, and I just wanted to say I'm doing OK." Somehow, I still don't think Pat believed that call. Guess I would just have to do better.

Another call went to the late Steve Snyder, owner of ParaFlite Parachute Company. His firm made the chute that malfunctioned. Receiving the same bit of disbelief, I informed Steve and (in my humble opinion) two properly placed rubber bands could have prevented the malfunction. That was noted and applied.

Hardly anyone would believe the parade of attorneys who visited the hospital room assuring me that "you can sue." Somehow I cannot in any fashion agree to sue someone when you make a parachute jump. Although it is now much safer than driving a car, it still isn't perfect. At Zephyrhills Parachute Center (2002) it was determined that there was one fatality every 65 thousand parachute jumps. And, frankly, some of those fatalities, nationally, could be attributed to pilot error, e.g. rapidly making high-speed corrections too close to terra firma. We in skydiving accept the risk of the sport and consider legal action an abomination.

The next day, the same phone allowed me to call NBC's Monitor radio program and give them a direct interview about the fall to earth. Monitor and NBC said it was the first time the interviewer and interviewee were the same person.

There's always something about a tragedy that brings out the best is people. September 11, 2001 proved that. At least it does provoke action. At the television station where I anchored the news, the station sales manager, Wes Quinn was doing some Sunday afternoon work when he heard about my big impression on the landscape.

Within minutes, he said, a television newsman who had earlier been released by the competing station called and said he was applying for your job." "What did you tell the would-be?" I wondered. "I told him," Quinn said, "that you weren't dead yet!" "Well," I added, "you can't blame a guy for being first in line." I never begrudged him his effort, but I didn't plan to die! I knew only too well the competitive nature of broadcasting. The subversion in broadcasting would put the KGB to shame.

When you're the anchor on the air, everyone wants your job. They even feel they could do a better job of anchoring the news.

Actually, I worked my way into radio, with a brief stint in the U.S. Air Force, and then returned to broadcasting and college in my little hometown nestled in the foothills of North Carolina. In between working 60 hours a week and going to college 18 hours per week, I started to raise a family as well. I started in a big way, for by the time I entered television in the Tampa-St. Petersburg, Florida market, I had two beautiful daughters and a son on the way. Later, we added another daughter... and much later, still another young lady.

You really appreciate your real friends when you're in the hospital. More than five thousand cards, letters and telegrams arrived, along with enough flowers to add to every room in the hospital. One lady wrote to me asking, "when you saw that neither one of your parachutes would work, why didn't you get back on the airplane?" I tried, lady, but flapping my arms as hard as possible, I still couldn't make it.

It was amazing, and smart television, when my closest competitor showed up at the hospital and did a 30 minute interview with me. To their credit, station WTVT, Channel 13 in Tampa ran medical reports each newscast. They really had more to say about the incident and covered it better than my own station. That meant, I suppose, I had to get back to work. My absence and the competitor's reports increased their rating share at the expense of my station.

Since I had passed the litmus test of survival for more than a week, plans were underway to transfer me from Winter Haven back to St. Joseph's Hospital in Tampa for continued therapy and rehabilitation. The sisters and nurses made sure I was well cared for, with a cold beer nightcap placed in my room each night. That was through the courtesy of a Senior Vice President of Eckerd Drugs, Headquartered in Clearwater, Florida. That man, Floyd Glisson, saw to it the Eckerd jet had room for a couple extra cold beers to be delivered to me in Tampa. Whatta man! He later became a sky diving aficionado and a life-long friend!

Putting my bones back together, I recall telling another prospective jumper, a gentleman by the name of Richard Bach, that skydiving is not without some perils. Having had the opportunity to serve as a skydiving mentor to this giant of an author I felt, as I would with any prospective student, I should point out the joy and the possible dangers. Bach, with the heart of a 20 year old and the wisdom that had to come from living hundreds of years, turned out to be a marvelous student. He made seven jumps on his first day of training, and those were the old cheapo parachutes, too! They did not let a 200-pound, 6' 6" person down lightly.

Richard Bach wrote about his experiences:

Richard Bach

"I kid him about it. Arch Deal, everybody else tells me skydiving is so safe and I don't believe them and you come along and say, 'Well this time the main came out in a ball and I cut away and opened the reserve and all the panels blew out and I figured I'd better get ready for a PLF (parachute landing fall)..' Is that any way to get somebody to go out for his first jump?" I kid him about that, but maybe it's a little bit true, maybe there's a part within that would despise me for walking a path because everybody says it's safe to follow."

"Then in the Parachute Ranch Cessna 182, and Mac McGraw opening the door for my first static line, shouting 'GET READY' over the wind. And in me there is this bespectacled horn-rimmed person with a sheaf of written arguments that one should be frightened, after all; what if, what if, what if, don't you understand, Richard? "

"But I'm no more than intellectually frightened. For I can see, out that door (GET OUT, Mac shouts), there's my sky, my same warm sky whom I have touched and who has touched me in so many ways, calling again a different way this time, saying hello once more."

"'Go!' he shouts and arch-thousand; two thousand...and she takes me and the airplane flies away; the airplane is gone and I'm alone in the sky!"

Bach continued: *"I'm a beginner still, but now at least I've hugged my sky at terminal (falling at 120 miles per hour), moved across her a bit, turning, and loved her the more for the fall and sound of her in my arms. I'm learning your strange language, and names of canopies and gear, but it's the same as airplane-flying is to pilots--not the rag and hardware that matters, but the sky out there, singing to us and saying hi, new every time the door swings open to her."*

"Someday, Arch Deal, I'll stand on the grass in my Frenchies (jump boots), root beer in hand, and I'll tell you calm about the time my main came out all in a ball, and I cut away, of course, and would you believe the reserve was just RAGS?"

"Obviously, however, since I'm standing here with this root beer, I had to use a little skill and daring ..."

Richard soon proved (as he did in flying) he was a natural. He became as expert in handling his parachute canopy as he was in handling his hangar filled with aircraft. They ranged from Pitts Specials to old rag wings that included a Dehaviland Rapide. This "Stranger to the Ground" embraced the air again and again until this master of thrilling books became a master of the sport of skydiving.

Unfortunately, the same guy who sort of talked him into the sport inadvertently talked him out of it. My "Big Bounce" may have slowed some enthusiasts while spurring on others. Richard said he began to think, 'what if, what if, what if, etc.' I always hoped that my return to the sky would always be a positive sign to others to never give up, to pursue their dreams; to get "back on the horse."

A groundsman at the Gardens, Johnny Gates, witnessed my bounce on that fateful day and solemnly swore he would never do that! Just as amazing, when I returned to Cypress Gardens one year later, he decided to take up skydiving and became a real expert and a legend in skydiving annals. Everyone in skydiving loved the friendliness and abilities of Johnny. On every jump he would shout to all the skydivers to have a good time and "don't f---ing die!" This legend was to break his own rule one day. During freefall, he had a massive coronary. Skydiving had nothing to do with it: it could have occurred watching a kiddies show.

Skydivers came from across the nation to honor Johnny and friendly chide his memory for "breaking his own rule!"

Back in my hospital bed, I vowed, "I shall return!" I probably saw too many movies about MacArthur. That sounds awfully heroic. It really isn't. It seemed to be the proper thing to say at the time. Later, it would haunt me. Now I was the interviewee and not the interviewer! The constant question would be, "Well, Arch, when are you going back to make that next BIG jump?" Talk about sweating bullets! I finally chose an answer that would succeed in boxing me in even further. "The next jump," I promised, "will be exactly one year after the big bounce."

My employer wasn't at all happy about that decision. WFLA-TV General Manager Bill Faber had questioned me on my fortieth birthday, "Well, since you've turned 40, you're going to give up sky diving, aren't you?" "No," I responded. "Why should I?" "Well," he quipped proudly, "when I turned 40, I gave up scuba diving!" "Gee," I said absent-mindedly, "glad you never talked to Jacques Cousteau."

He probably never appreciated that comment and it was one of my best! Many people feel that skydivers have a death wish. That just isn't true. As a group, they probably love life as much or more than anyone I know. One skydiver put it, "We don't fear death as much as the fear of never having lived."

So, relations at the television station began to fade a bit. Adding to that, the station, owned by the town's only newspaper, refused to pay my medical expenses even though I was on assignment for the station. In fact, when I was first transferred to the hospital, the Tribune's insurance manager called to say, "He isn't covered by insurance."(WFLA-TV was owned by The Tampa Tribune). Proof that this was an endorsed promotion for the station was evidenced by the public services announcements that the station ran inviting spectators to go to Cypress Gardens, watch the skydiving and get an autograph.

As I said earlier, I detest lawsuits; therefore, I turned down countless offers from attorneys who paraded by my hospital bed and encouraged me to go for the "big bucks." All I wanted was the medical insurance I paid for and to which I was entitled. It turned out to be a bit nasty. With every court decision, the Tribune Company was ordered to pay. They appealed, lost, appealed, lost, appealed and lost. In all, it dragged on nine years in efforts to keep from paying a paltry 20 thousand in medical fees. Can you imagine, only twenty thousand bucks. Today, my medical bills would have soared over a million.   They paid as a last resort and I found myself in less than disfavor, in spite of winning the rating battles for over 15 consecutive years.

Chapter 18
Change of Stations

Then ABC Network affiliate WTSP-TV in St. Petersburg offered to hire me as a combination news anchor and news director. I accepted this fresh challenge and to a large extent carried some of my viewers along with me. Channel 8, meanwhile, fell to a poor second in the ratings, heading for last place. There was some joy in Mudville after all.

Working with Channel 10 was an interesting and rewarding challenge. As news director and major on-air anchor, I had a great challenge… and I even found time to get to my other loves: flying and skydiving.

And as I got closer to the one-year anniversary of my bounce, I knew I had to prepare!

First of all, you cannot legally make a demonstration jump into a tight area without having at least one jump for practice during the past year. With that in mind, I drove to the Riverview, Florida drop zone to make my one proficiency jump. It came off without a hitch and I kept that one quiet. Cypress Gardens was (according to the media) to be my first jump since the impact on June 22, 1975!

Return to Cypress Gardens

But now, my heart wasn't in it. My drive for television news had been tempered somewhat by the infighting and my head was still in the clouds. I needed to go back to Cypress Gardens and jump again. The anniversary date was less than six months away and I was still hurting! There's an old cliché that states: when you're hurting, the only person who really cares you wouldn't tell!

Unfortunately, with human nature most people don't really care when they ask, "How are you?" There are even a few who might delight in your pains. You certainly wouldn't want to give them the satisfaction. Our news operation was moving along smoothly as we added the Bay Area's first ENG: Electronic News Gathering equipment. That's video for short. Prior to that time, everybody used the old Bell and Howell 16mm cameras and Auricon cameras for sound bites. It all changed as news gathering raced into the 20th Century. Suddenly, you never knew who was videotaping your exploits or your misadventures.

Moving closer to my date with destiny, the various news media organizations were making their arrangements to cover my auspicious return to Cypress Gardens. There was almost a fatal hitch in the plans when the Gardens began to get "cold feet" and worried about a true repeat performance. Naturally their attorneys began to worry, what if, what if, what if? After firmly being reminded of their obligations, they acquiesced and our plans continued.

The competing station that provided so much coverage during my sojourn in the hospital asked for permission to accompany me in the jump plane; a request I could hardly refuse. My pilot, Bud Clark, was less than thrilled. He didn't like the prospect of carrying my body on another possible repeat performance.

Imagine the same parachute, the same airplane and the same reluctant pilot. It not only made for a good story but I wouldn't have had it any other way.

There was one change, however. The old parachute that had malfunctioned on me was being placed in a new container. A fellow by the name of Bill Booth, a gentleman with a flowing black beard that made you think he sold cough drops instead of parachute paraphernalia provided me with his new container system.

This genius of parachute design moved from Miami (where he was a school teacher) to Deland, Florida, where he perfected some of the most outstanding improvements in parachuting. Among those achievements was a release system that enabled the skydiver to get rid of a faulty parachute before opening another one. That was a very important step. I remember how my old releases had failed me on that fateful day, just a year earlier. Booth came to the drop zone and made adjustments on his new design and I prepared for a return to the Gardens.

Talk about a crowd, this was one of Cypress Gardens' most successful days. The place was absolutely packed. Obviously with folks waiting to see a successful parachute jump! Right? Hardly! It compares somewhat to the crowds at a NASCAR race. North Carolina was the hotbed of that type of stock car competition and I grew up with it. In fact, my father was an official scorer, keeping track of the rounds each car made and logging the pit stops.

Later, my father was honored as the "First Racing Father of the Year." That honor was bestowed at the Darlington, SC 500 Race, September 1, 1961! What an honor, especially since the only racing his sons did was in a "celebrity race" at the Hickory, NC Speedway. I was given the key to a modified race car from a gentleman who built it himself. He said, "I want you to win the race or blow the engine trying!" He really didn't mean that! I was leading everyone when the engine blew! So much for my racing skills!

I did, as a newsman, get a ride around the track at the Daytona International Speedway with former Daytona winner Marvin Panch at the wheel! I sat on the floor pan, no seat, no seatbelt, no helmet, as Marvin took me around the track at close to 180 miles per hour. The light poles went by like toothpicks in a bowl. What a thrill, until one of the officials noticed me in the car and ordered me out! He probably saved my life!

Having watched a lot of NASCAR races, I knew something about what the crowd was looking for. This was the same sort of crowd that packed into the Gardens. And the media was at the top of the pack. Each station, network and the print media wanted a piece of the action: a chance to see a "highly successful" return!!! To capture the "impact" of the landing, one station even set up a camera to record the event in slow motion. Wow, would I ever have liked to see that in slow motion. Unfortunately, to this day no one has come forth with a picture of my fall to earth. Imagine if that impact had occurred in the time of mini-cams and instant replay!

Channel 13, the competing station during my rapid trip to the ground, had requested an opportunity to send a reporter in the jump plane for my return match. How could I refuse a chance to get more coverage, and from the opposition? It was a good clean rivalry at a time when sensationalism had not soared to excessive heights. My new station, Channel 10, afforded total coverage of the event and the other cameras remained on the ground waiting for the exit.

My plan, as before, was to fly over Lake Eloise, check the winds, exit at 3500 feet, and open my parachute, as intended before, at 2,000 feet above the Gardens. Those best laid plans were to go a bit askew.

As pilot Bud Clark rotated the Cessna 182 off the hot, muggy grass airstrip, the cumulus clouds of Florida were beginning to build. On a typical summer day you can count on the build-up to start early and continue until the cumulus amasses into the huge nimbo culumus that often become anvil head thunderstorms. This was now happening.

As we flew over the lake, moments from exit, the lower clouds were beginning to move into the area and the approach of a heavy thunderstorm was imminent. It was obvious that my planned exit at 3500 feet would not be possible. That presented an immediate potential problem. The chute was packed for a "terminal" opening. That meant I would have to fall a good 10 seconds to get it to open properly. Unfortunately, my maximum altitude, scraping the bottom of the clouds, would be barely over two thousand feet, which just happens to be the minimum legal opening altitude for an expert parachutist. This meant I would have to open the chute right out the door of the aircraft. There could be no time for freefall to build up speed for a clean opening. The only alternative would be a high-speed exit. Crank up the airplane to its maximum speed with the door removed, bomb out the door and pull like hell!

Within minutes, even the 2,000 feet would be gone and the jump would have to be canceled. It's now or never. To the pilot, I yelled over the engine noise, "Bud, thanks again for the ride!" As Jacques Cousteau would say, "See you below." With a nod and a forced smile to my onboard camera companions I climbed briefly onto the step of the Cessna. Then I was gone! With a lump the size of a football in my throat, I soared again in the wind, feeling again the air and the freedom of spirit. Unfortunately, I was also feeling the tiny voice within that said, "What if, what if, what if?"

Only a second from the airplane (that seemed like 30 from the rush of adrenaline), I threw out the pilot chute to start to opening. Expecting the worst, I began to experience a bit of it. Instead of a firm tug of the opening, there was the flutter of what skydivers call a "snivel," a super slow opening that sometimes doesn't open at all. Actually, they usually open, but you can't just look at it all the way to the ground expecting something to happen. 'Oh, now,' I thought, 'not again. Come on, baby, you can do it, open, open, open.' Then, the canopy began to breathe life and slowly unfold. What a beautiful sight. It probably took an extra 500 feet, but it was open and flying. 'Wow,' I thought, 'what a rush, this is too much fun!'

Below, the slow opening had really captured the attention of the camera crews who spiritedly moved into action. The opening of the chute must have prompted an "Aw shucks," from the crews. I thought, 'Surely somebody is going to demand their money back!' Oh well, the chute opened and began flying, flying beautifully over Lake Eloise and headed for the bright, white sand glistening by the spectators.

The roar of the crowd was deafening and inspiring as I made that final approach over the water and landed, just a tad short, in six inches of water. I went to my knees for a moment on touchdown. Some probably thought I had fallen. Nope! I was just grateful for the return and the ability to make it on that beautiful day. My back was still grinding and crunching a bit from a year earlier, but who cares. It was getting better each day. And, I was back!

The film company shooting slow motion offered to give me the film - said they couldn't use it now. My head was still in the clouds, which now were descending and turning ominously black. Sure enough, rain, accompanied by high, gusty winds was on the way. Everyone was pulling away from the area and many were headed back to their cars.

Flying back to Tampa (I had flown over in a rented aircraft) I had to dodge the thunderheads. Back on land and driving for home, I received my first indication that the public was aware of my return jump.

A gentleman of Hispanic descent pulled alongside my car, rolled down his window, stuck out his hands like the Allstate ad and shouted "Cajones, cajones!" It was a while later before I learned what that meant. It was appreciated, but it was just something I had to do.

Back to work! I still had an evening newscast to prepare, but a lot of my work was already "in the can" as they say in broadcast journalism. Filmed, videotaped and ready for replay. Since I made up a good portion of the news I decided to take the evening off and hand over the anchor duties to Marshall Cleaver, an accomplished, smooth anchorman with an uncommon mastery of the English language.

This time I played couch potato and watched the newscasts. I always joked that watching yourself on TV was almost akin to visual masturbation. Sometimes you had to do it just to catch your own mistakes. Just never get to the point that you like what you see. If you do, you're in trouble!

Watching Channel 13 and the newsman of color who accompanied me in the aircraft was particularly amusing. He did an excellent job but when he told the audience, "Arch Deal was absolutely calm, cool and collected when he climbed out of the airplane!" I almost fell off the couch. 'Boy,' I thought, 'I sure fooled him!'

Perhaps that comes with too many years as a news anchor, where you mask your emotions and just present facts to the audience. Under my jumpsuit, my heart was pounding and the adrenaline was flowing, but I tried to present a cool impression like the late great Peter Jennings.

The Miller "Six Pack in the Sky" skydiving team

Chapter 18
The Six Pack

Returning to my anchor duties, I soon found that I was drifting off to Zephyrhills on the weekends and putting my "knees in the breeze" as often as possible.

Working with the Florida Citrus Commission, I had planned to make 40 jumps in one day just to celebrate my birthday. It all went smoothly, with my body hurling out the door of a vintage Cessna 195 once every 9 minutes and 30 seconds. I sipped Florida Gold between every jump. The only problem I had was I began to slosh around toward the end of the day. Jim Haerer, a former Vietnam F-4 fighter pilot, was at the control of the Cessna which he dived toward the runway each time I left the door.

Not content with that, I decided to do 50 jumps in one day the next year. That was a mistake! Lots of folks said, "Wow, the ten years just flew back, Arch!" I thought perhaps I should have made 100 jumps. Maybe no one would think I'm 100. But, then again! This time, I was able to depart the Cessna 195 once every 6 minutes and 20 seconds. We used a golf cart to drive me from the target to the Cessna and waiting pilot, Jim Haerer.

Would you believe jump number 13 of the 50 was a malfunction? It went 'round and 'round and I chopped it away! Those are skydiving words for releasing the main chute. The reserve opened without hesitation and in two minutes I was on the ground, strapping on another chute and heading for the aircraft again. My crew of five was packing the chutes. I jokingly kidded them about the extra thrill they packed into number 13! "No more, please!"

Boy, did we ever party that night! The beer flowed along with the "war" stories of close calls and exciting jumps... like, "you'd never believe how low I was before it finally opened."

That love of flying never left. To continue both sports, the thrill of flying and the thrill of free fall, I bought an airplane. It was my first Cessna 182. It was a beauty, even though it had many years of flight in her logs. She was built in 1960, but with a healthy engine overhaul and a fresh coat of very expensive paint (the acrylic type) she was back in the air. This particular model was probably the most famous first jump vehicle. Almost every skydiver (in the early days at least) made their first free fall out of this lumbering tricyle-gear high winged aircraft. Legally it was certified to carry four jumpers and, of course, the pilot.

Usually jump altitude was no more than 7,500 feet above terra firma. That would give you a 30-second freefall. That was equal to one mile plummeting through the air before whipping out the ripcord and opening the chute. So I set up operation at the "Sod Firm" west of Brandon, Florida. It was so named for at certain times of the year the field was used to grow sod which would be cut into squares and sold to home builders. Only in places like Florida do you get "instant" lawn. All you have to do is water it and kill the cinch bugs that'll eat all the roots if they get the chance.

Initially, it started as a place to train the skydiving professional team… where we could practice without interruption. At least that was the way it started.

Suddenly other wannabes would show up to make their first jump. Most of my performers were certified instructors so we got into the student business as well. Between practicing with the team I would fly loads with students and their jumpmasters.

Practicing at the local drop zone with my "pick up" demo team, a lady jumper by the name of Linda Hale had a suggestion. I had signed a contract with Anheuser-Busch Company to produce a skydiving team to perform nationally. We had five canopies, logoed Budweiser, Busch, Michelob, Michelob Light and Natural Light. Linda suggested, "If you had another canopy you could call your team the Six Pack."

From that came the registered Trade Mark "The Six Pack in the Sky™" The sixth canopy, incidentally, was the Anheuser-Busch, "A" and Eagle.

We ran a two-year contract with Busch, performing into Busch Stadium in St Louis (always wanted to get a picture of myself by the big sign that says, "This way to Arch") and various racetracks across the country.

About the time the contract was about to expire, I began a courtship with Miller Brewing Company, the firm that shocked every brewery by producing the hottest selling Lite Beer in the world, Miller Lite. Barry Barrett, brand manager for Lite, was interested in the Six Pack and I was definitely interested in departing Busch's organization. You might say, "I saw the Lite—Lite Beer from Miller!"

Page 90

Barrett proposed I produce one canopy to perform at the annual Spring Break at Daytona Beach and Fort Lauderdale, Florida. Done! Within weeks, the canopy was flying and I was on my way to Daytona.

Quickly, I found that beach jumps during Spring Break could be extremely hazardous. First, you don't look at the bikini-clad girls until after you land. Second, you must resist temptation. Walking away from one of my first jumps a small, sexy voice cooed over my shoulder, "I'll give you anything you want for that T-shirt, anything at all." Darn it, one look and I knew she meant it. Worse that than, she was a gorgeous blonde with all the trimmings in a suit that almost fit. Still worse than that, it was the only skydiving T-Shirt I had brought with me, so it wouldn't be possible to yield to that temptation without trouble. Explain to the wife what happened to your shirt. You won't win! Anyway, that's not the way to win points for your sponsor (or your wife).

The practice and the training of students went very well. However, you soon learned that you do not get holidays. After all, holidays are when all the skydivers head to the drop zone and get their "knees in the breeze."

Hundreds and hundreds of hours flying brings about the old adage, "There are old pilots and there are bold pilots. But there are no old, bold pilots." There's a reason for that old expression. My old Cessna, as nice as she was, did have a problem. In a "bad" landing long before she became my property, she was damaged. That damage included the nose gear assembly. Apparently, the shaft had been bent and re-straightened. Occasionally, taking off from the sod air field, a bump would send the shaft upwards where it would sometimes stick. If this happened, it was very disconcerting. Not because it was up, but because that which goes up must come down.

Unfortunately, that would usually happen when you are cruising along at altitude, then BAM!! Suddenly all the jumpers want to get out of the airplane which now sounds like it was in a mid-air collision. You have to understand, sky divers usually don't trust airplanes. They are a means to an end: a device to get them to altitude so they can skydive. Once when clouds obscured the drop zone, I had to descend and land with a full load of jumpers. When this would happen someone would invariably ask, "Can we land with all of us in the plane?" Yes! And there is a Santa Claus.

There was one particular time when the gear did not plop back down and instead was canted off to the left. When on the ground, a tricycle-gear aircraft is steered by turning the nose gear with the pedals. Push right to go right, left to go left. Attempting to land at the Sod Field after dropping a load of jumpers, I made my usual approach to land. When the nose gear touched the field it suddenly threw the Cessna into a sharp right turn and into the edge of a barbed-wire fence. Not good! Suddenly the gear collapsed and the plane was on its nose with the left wing stuck in the barbed-wire. So remembering how to do the right thing, I cut the Master Switch, turned off the fuel mixture switch to the right of my seat, and dove out of the grounded Cessna. When I got out, I found fuel was spurting under the cowling but there was no fire. But the bird was bent and to a pilot that is one of the saddest things you'll ever see. She would not fly again until the nose gear was replaced. Along with the cowling, a new prop bent when she nosed over. Again, however, I escaped with no injuries—with the exception of a shattered pride. It was just one of my many, many narrow escapes. There are those who feel I'm trying to outdo the nine lives of a cat!

Chapter 19
Venimos con Amistad

Puerto Rico is a beautiful Island. It was certainly exciting when Miller Brewing called me to perform over San Juan with the Miller High Life Skydiving Team. Our motto was "venimos con Amistad." In all, we actually took to the sky to perform six times and even found time to give sky diving instructions to a famed Puerto Rican TV entertainer, Lusito Vigoro.

This turned out to be exciting in more ways than one. Our freefall photographer Dave Floyd, known as "Pink Floyd," was among our jumpers as we decided to chronicle the event in free fall. The entire training sequence was videotaped over Ponce, on the southwest coast of Puerto Rico. Our airborne trip to the jump site took us over the gorgeous rain forests of the island.

That Saturday evening, the entire team appeared on San Juan television in a three-hour extravaganza of music and entertainment. Within the show, Lusito talked about his aerial adventures and invited the public to come out the next day and watch the team perform over Alambique Beach, a favorite spot for the Puerto Rican sun worshippers.

As usual, the weather was beautiful as we loaded our jump gear and boarded the twin Beech aircraft. The old D-18 growled and rumbled through the air but did the job fairly well, if you could escape the noise.

It's the same type of aircraft that used to have problems with the wings falling off. Seems like with lots of airtime, the vibration caused some of the wing spars to crack. Not a good thing at all!

It was the same type that folk rocker Jim Croce was traveling in when the wings did depart. Tragedy causes a lot of things to get fixed; cars, airplanes and parachutes alike.

The sun sparkled over the Caribbean and the white caps were just beginning to build on the surface as we dropped our wind indicators and started to climb to 8500 feet above the San Juan International Airport. What a day! The crowds were already dotting the white sand of the beach, and it was obvious there was going to be lots of spectators for our show.

My Spanish, limited to ordering chicken, black beans and yellow rice (arroz con pollo con frioles negroes), caused to me ask Lusito to narrate the show. I would start off with a few choice, well-memorized Spanish greetings, then the master of the language would continue. After all, he already had one jump under his belt and was fast becoming an expert.

We lined up the Beechcraft on jump run and everyone was psyched and ready to go. They included, with Pink and me; Billy Weber, an ace performer formerly from Michigan where he grew up on his father's drop zone; and Steve Wilson, a paramedic from Brooksville, Florida. Steve and I were about to have a great day!

The plan was to dive out of the Beech and open our chutes within three seconds to start building the "stack." Our trademark, Six Pack in the Sky™, consisted of carefully flying the six parachutes together. We started out by diving the second chute toward the backside of the jumper under chute number one. Ideally, I ran the leading edge of my parachute into Wilson's backside, and he grabbed hold. Then, he locked his feet into the centerlines of the chute and slid down to place his feet in "keepers" between the risers of my parachute. Then number three contacted me, and I began to slide down his lines.

This continued until all six were thus hooked together. It is a safe maneuver, if is done carefully. If not, you could become a statistic, or at least be in for an incredibly wild ride.

Those tried and true methods were not to be applied this day. As I flew my Glide Path Manta parachute toward Wilson, inexplicably, he turned into my face. Wow, the closing speed of those two chutes could reach 40 miles per hour. The right side of his canopy hit the left side of mine and both of us were sent spiraling. However, both chutes regained their composure and we tried again. This time, as I approached, Steve again hooked his canopy to face mine. This pass, however, was not to have us spinning away from each other. The moment the canopies collided, the right side of his chute collapsed the left side of mine, causing the right side of my chute (the only part still flying) to immediately wrap around Wilson.

It should be pointed out that "wraps," as we call them, only get worse. They go from bad to worse to well, you don't want to think about it. Worse case scenario is that he would be totally wrapped in my chute like a mummy or a burial shroud!

In cases like this, we try to talk to each other as rapidly as possible to decide and take the proper course of action. It was obvious the longer I stayed with Steve Wilson, the grimmer his fate. "Steve!" I shouted, "we're wrapped (no stuff, Sherlock!), and I've got to cut away!" "Go ahead!" Steve yelled back, "we've got a bad one going." Later Steve said he was confident that I knew what I was doing and that everything would be all right! Boy, if he only knew! It was my first and only wrap and it was a very scary thing.

Above us, ace skydiver Billy Weber, who wrote the textbook on packing parachutes, could be heard to shout, "That's a real one!" Pink, at the same time, was shooting pictures of the wildly gyrating parachutes that looked like so much garbage in the sky. Those pictures would later confirm what we suspected at the moment. The longer I stayed with this mess, the more the chute and line would wrap up Steve. I looked down, saw the cutaway handle and yanked like hell. With the fierce tug of centrifugal force from the spinning chutes, I was spewed away from the tangle of nylon and tracking off like some discarded rocket. I found the reserve ripcord and fired it off, opening a beautiful square reserve canopy. I probably muttered to myself, "Oh my God, it's open. I'm not going to be part of the Puerto Rican landscape after all."

Wilson, meanwhile, was in a mess. The lines of my canopy were still wrapped about him. For such instances, we carry hook-knives; very sharp instruments for such occasions. They can hook over a line and sever it like a hot knife through butter. This, Wilson was executing with blazin' speed. Perhaps too much speed! He chopped away six lines from the remains of my parachute wrapped about him and fell free from the mess. Accelerating clear, Wilson unloaded his reserve which opened flawlessly.

Our approach to the target was over tall palms to land on a narrow strip of Alambique Beach; a narrow strip made even smaller by the fact we were now under reserve canopies, which don't perform quite as well as the main chutes. Within half a minute, however, we were touching down on the intended target without further incident.

Talk about a couple of happy guys. The jettisoned chutes were recovered from the Caribbean by a police boat. Those officers were rewarded with mucho cervezas fria (much cold beer-Miller, of course).

On the ground, Weber sauntered up to Wilson, dangling the deployment bag of Wilson's reserve parachute. In his haste to slash through the lines, Steve had also severed the bridle to the reserve pilot chute. You're not supposed to do that! Nevertheless, it worked beautifully.

Steve always remembered every little detail of that horrific meeting in the sky over the beautiful island in the Caribbean.

That evening, there was much celebration under the Puerto Rican moon. Wilson, who was grateful for the hook knife I included with each rig, had a jeweler fashion for me a gold miniature hook knife tie tack. There's an old custom in skydiving that deems when a reserve saves your life, the one who packed it should receive a case of beer or a bottle of his choice. For the reserve I had packed, Steve presented me with a bottle of Royal Salute Premiere Scotch. He was a gentleman…and a skydiver!

Miller proved to be a great sponsor and soon I found I was not only providing up to 100 shows per year for them but I also became a member of the exclusive All Stars: Elite sports professionals who hawked the Miller Lite Brand.

Actually, I felt a little out of place. Here I was in a group with people like Ben Davidson (6'9" Oakland Raider), Dick Butkus, All-Pro Ray Nitschke and the late great mystery writer Mickey Spillane, a very prolific writer who introduced "Mike Hammer" to readers.

Mickey, a long-time South Carolina resident, was accompanied on his All Star Appearances by Lee Meredith. Lee, a New Jersey born beauty, was an actress, one of the prettiest All-Stars and one of only two women. The other was Lori Bowen Rice, posing here with Olympian Longjump Champion Bob Beamon, the author, and former Dallas Cowboy D. D. Lewis on a Miller Lite "All Star Cruise."

Working with Boog Powell was always a pleasure. Boog was built like a football linebacker and I found at an All Star meeting outside Denver, on a rainy night, that I could not exceed his Lite Beer capacity. Born John Wesley Powell in Lakeland, Florida, he was a former first baseman in Major League Baseball who played for the Baltimore Orioles. Boog played a total of 17 years in the big leagues, fourteen of those with Baltimore. One of the most beloved Orioles, he says he still signs about 500 autographs a night. Bob Uecker and Dick Williams; basketball greats Red Auerbach, Buck Buchanan; the irrepressible Boom-Boom Geoffrion; sports writer Frank Deford; and, of course, there was the big guy John Madden. Madden was one of history's great football coaches and without a doubt one of the very best commentators on the pigskin game. He always questioned my sanity as a skydiver.

Madden, you probably have heard, preferred not to fly. Maybe it's because there isn't anything big enough to hold him. After all, would anyone jump out of a perfectly good airplane? After thousands of hours as a commercial pilot, I can say I have never seen a perfectly good airplane. I have, however, seen thousands of safe ones. The get-togethers we had were phenomenal. It was the greatest ad campaign in the history of beer, and probably one of the greatest campaigns, period!

Bob Uecker, referred to as Mister Baseball, was one of the greatest comics of all time. This guy was full of jokes at 3 am. As a speaker, I decided long ago that I would be happy and honored to introduce and do the lead-in to Bob Uecker or Bob Hope. Not on your life would I follow either one! At the Beverly Hilton one night, an agency "rep" tried to do his own comedy routine after Uecker. He died a thousand horrible deaths before the hook pulled him from the stage. Uecker has completed 28 seasons as the club's number one announcer. He earned the 2003 Ford C. Frick Award and will forever be recognized in Baseball's Hall of Fame in Cooperstown, New York. On July 27, 2003, he made one of the most memorable speeches in Hall of Fame induction history.

He was one of the most popular of the Miller Lite All-Stars in commercials for Lite Beer from Miller. Uecker was cast as a radio announcer in the film Major League, which was filmed at County Stadium, along with the sequel, Major League II. He launched a TV acting career in ABC's sitcom Mr. Belvedere. One-hundred-twenty-two episodes went into syndication. He was one of Johnny Carson's favorite guests and made some 100 appearances on the Tonight Show.

As mentioned, this was an honorable group of great athletes. How did I fit it? Well, fortunately, the group also included Corky Carroll, three-time World Surfing Champ. As a skydiver, I could relate to that. Corky and I were sort of on the outer fringes, each "hanging ten" in a different way. He found his thrill riding the surf, while I preferred to "surf" the sky.

New Orleans: Pre Katrina

Before the onslaught of Hurricane Katrina smacked onto the coast of Louisiana and Mississippi, I had the extreme pleasure of skydiving over the city of New Orleans a dozen times, for Mardi Gras and for the French Quarter Festival. Besides immensely enjoying the Cajun food and fantastic Dixieland jazz, it was just a fun place to be and the target was one of the most sporting you can imagine.

My first jump for the Mardi Gras had as my target Louis Armstrong Park. There, you only had to miss the huge oak trees, power lines and people. First touching down, an officer came up to me and said he would have to arrest me for the skydive. Calmly, I pulled out my authorization papers and proved the jump was fully sanctioned by the city and the Federal Aviation Authority.

"Man, that was a fine jump!" the officer exclaimed… and we became fast friends. In fact, he gave me one of the infamous "Get out of Jail Free cards." Heck, I thought it was a Monopoly card. "No!" explained the officer. "If you get arrested for anything short of a felony, just show the card and you walk!" Sounds incredulous, but I have been assured that it was a real thing well known by the folks along the bayous.

For the French Quarter Festival, the weather was more pleasant in mid April, and the target was moved to Decatur Street in the French Quarter. Now, talk about a sporting target: we had the Mississippi River just south of us, huge power lines between us and the river (power enough to contact electricity through nylon) and Jackson Square very close to the north. It is surrounded by a steel-spiked fence, with Andrew Jackson raising his sword in the center of the park. Outside were tens of thousands of people, horse drawn carriages and to the west, Jackson Brewery.

Seems strong winds were always blowing over the brewery and one caught me in a downdraft, slamming me onto Decatur Street. NFL quarterback and Louisiana favorite Bert Jones (as well as a Miller Lite All-Star) was my "ground man" holding a windsock to indicate the direction of the winds.

In a split second, Bert raced up to me and asked if I was OK! "Bert," I replied, "you know as a quarterback how to take a 'hit'. Sometimes you do a tip-toe landing, other times you roll with it." I decided to rename the street De-crater Street. We had a dozen landings on that famous street. It was a time I will never forget: a very sporting target, but we (The Six Pack in the Sky) were always on target. We felt a very close kinship with New Orleans and the French Quarter, which was built well above sea level.

I had occasion to perform over the "Big Easy" in the company of my very close friends, two doctors and two of the warmest and most intelligent people I have had the honor of knowing: Drs. Richard and Angela Rasmussen.

Doctors Angela and Richard Rasmussen

Angela, by the way, is a former Mrs. Florida, an appropriate title for a very pretty and accomplished lady. The first time we were there was in April of 1990. At that time, Dr. Rick was my ground man, holding the windsock in the center of Decatur Street. As happens, more often than not, Rick got the urge to try skydiving. Angela (to get it out of his system) asked me to arrange the first jump for her husband - a mistake! That first jump turned into a couple thousand! Frankly, I have never seen anyone excel so readily in any endeavor, whether as a surgeon, skydiver or pilot. He's also a whiz on the computer.

On that trip, Dr. Angela realized she was expecting her fourth child. With three sons, Ricky Junior, Matt and Marc, she was expecting her first daughter, Kirstin.

The purpose of this vignette came about 19 years later when my friends treated me to a return trip to the Big Easy, New Orleans and the French

Quarter. Moving forward from his skydiving, Dr. Rick has flown with me many times as I reported traffic for radio in the Tampa Bay Area. He showed talent as a pilot and progressed through all the stages from private pilot with instrument, commercial and sea plane ratings.

We flew to New Orleans in his new Cirrus sleek aircraft: a marvel of workmanship. It was complete with the most sophisticated digital instrument panel backed by a second digital and an analog system. It had air-conditioning, de-icing and even a parachute as a last resort life-saving device.

Years later, I had a dance with Kirstin, now a beautiful young lady with a matching personality. We had an occasion to dance at a Krewe of Venus party arranged by Dr. Rick, Past King of Venus and President of the Krewe. Man, does that ever make you feel old.

It was great to see the progress being made in New Orleans and the French Quarter. People were returning to savor the food, music and culture of the area. It has a long way to go…but is making progress!

Chapter 20
Flying Traffic

At about the same time, a salesman for a local radio station approached me. "What are you doing," he asked, "each morning between 6:45 and 9:00?" Like most "normal" people, I was getting an extra hour of sack time, then hitting the deck for a shower, shave and coffee.

"Well," the red-headed salesman asked, "how would you like to fly and report on traffic conditions each morning over Tampa Bay?" I must admit, the thought never occurred to me! As a pilot and anchorman, I could combine the two!

Quickly, the deal was cemented, and I hopped a commercial jet out to Tulsa to pick up a spanking new Cessna 152. It's the sort of aircraft you "wear." It's that small. Room for two, if you're good friends. Talk about close. For a couple of those years, I flew with a passenger, a petite blonde who has since become a successful radio personality. Sitting that close together, my right tricep and her left breast were always together. But, that was no "big deal." If she had been equipped like Dolly Parton, there wouldn't have been room for us in the plane. Did I say the plane was small? You had to step outside to change your mind.

In the course of flying and amassing over 20,000 hours and close to two million miles in that little Cessna, I had more than my share of close calls. Probably one of the more outstanding was the case of a Boeing 727 (the name of the airline will remain my secret) that was headed for a landing at Tampa International. Concurrently, I was landing on cross-runways. That meant I would cross over the approach end of his runway (36 left heading north) about the time he would be touching down. No Problem! That would put him about a thousand feet below me. While on the downwind to land, the station's afternoon host called for a traffic report, which I was giving at the same time. Launching into the report, I glanced under my left wing and saw the 727 heading straight for me. Again, no problem! He was descending for his runway. Continuing my report, I continued to glance under my wing. Apparently, my delivery was becoming more pedantic by the second. Hey, wait a minute; this guy isn't getting any lower. He's heading right for me - me in my little tiny Cessna! Suddenly, in my headset I heard the 727 pilot shout to the tower, "I can't get down, gotta go round!"

Talk about moving, I crammed the yoke of my Cessna to the panel, pointing it straight down to the ground. At the same time, I looked up to count the rivets of this monster machine crossing right over where I had been a second before. 'Needs its belly washed,' I thought as the behemoth roared through my airspace.

Closing the throttle on my tiny craft, I eased the controls back to get out of the "much higher airspeed than this plane is built for" and banked sharply for my approach to the cross runway. That continued without incident. After all, what else could go wrong? Within seconds, my wheels touched down on Runway 9 (facing east). Rolling out, I departed on a taxiway and called the tower. "Any problems with that near miss?" I queried. "None at all," replied the relieved voice in the tower, "unless you want to file on (report) the pilot of the 727." "No way," I continued, "just as long as some little old lady doesn't report to the media, 'that little airplane almost killed us all.'" "So noted," the tower added, "Good Flying!" Flying hell, it was just good getting out of the way!

It wasn't, by far, the only close encounter. There were many more to be accounted for while flying over a million miles over the Tampa Bay area. One of them was the final approach of a huge 747 Jumbo Jet. Realizing he was too high for final approach, the pilot reluctantly told the tower, "I'm too high, gotta go round." That was all the encouragement I needed to scamper for cover and avoid the wash of one of the biggest machines ever to occupy air space. Imagine the fuel for a go-round for a 747. It was equal to a high-paid executive's yearly salary.

During the continuing years, there were occasions when I could have sworn I came close enough to other aircraft to get the color of the pilot's eyes. But, close is only good in hand grenades and horseshoes!

One of the closest encounters was with a small Brazilian aircraft flown by PBI, a small commuter airline. Making a straight-in approach to runway 27 (which faces west), I was cleared to land by Tampa Air Traffic Control. However, my peripheral vision told me another aircraft, a Banderante (small two-engine turboprop), was approaching the same runway on a dogleg approach; that's an angled approach, not straight in. "Tampa Tower," I queried, "how about the 'Bandit' on my right?" "Disregard the Bandit," said the tower, "you're cleared to land." Well, it was obvious the Bandit was not talking or listening to anyone. He had tunnel vision toward the airfield. With an impact imminent, I suddenly broke to the left and climbed to avoid the bandit, which glided under me and touched down on the runway. Suddenly, the tower came to life, "Arch One, thanks for the avoidance maneuver. We'll be talking with the Bandit pilot whenever he gets on frequency!"

Through four engines, four complete paint schemes and countless close calls, the little Cessna served me well. I would go off almost each weekend and sky dive for Miller, return home and hop into the Cessna to report the traffic.

As you already know, the close calls in the sky were not only in an airplane, but also at times under a parachute...

Miller had me traveling about a half million miles per year. That required some coordination. Somewhere along the way, I met a young lady from Yorkshire, England. She had that million dollar smile, one of the most beautiful personalities you have ever encountered, and a face and figure to match. Somehow, I knew I was in trouble. Along with that potent combination, she possessed a remarkable ability to book airline passage better than anyone I had ever met in the travel business. Coincidentally, her name, Karen, was the same as my oldest daughter. Immediately, my travel business picked up and so did my interest in Karen. After all, man does not live by skydives alone. The inevitable occurred. Karen followed me across the nation to performances, paying her own way to be with me. Soon, we became an inseparable pair. As they say, "love is blind, but the neighbors aren't."

My travel bookings were infallible until, alas, Mum decided to return to Jolly 'old England and take her offspring along. My travel plans ran aground like a ship tossed into the reefs. My assigned travel agent worked out of the basement of a nursing home in Milwaukee. To say the least, the arrangement was unique and the bookings were something else. One trip to upstate New York had us returning to Tampa through Nova Scotia.

My phone bill was beginning to look like the national debt, even before Bill Clinton. Karen and I spent more than an hour a day on the phone from Tampa to England. This was expensive! Finally, I decided to go after her. I had envisioned an Officer and a Gentleman scenario where I sweep her off her feet and carry her through the Heathrow Terminal. Finally, I arrived, with the Delta L-1011 touching down on the tarmac, January 2, 1987. Fighting my way through Customs, I spied the young lady standing in the center of the aisle, clutching her overnight bag. Our eyes met, frozen for a moment in the job of being away from each other for six months. The reaction was immediate: Karen got sick and rushed to the ladies room.

Afterwards, we spent a wonderful weekend in London's Hyde Park Hilton, just behind Buckingham Palace. You wouldn't have thought London would be so romantic.

We returned to Tampa, were married in my home, and produced one of the most beautiful babies you've ever seen - a daughter named Michelle Marie. That turned out to be the high point of the entire twelve years.

Performing over Clearwater, Florida's Air Park, the American Fall Guy's Parachute Team (my generic team) was just starting to stack up the parachutes into a four-pack. In this maneuver, we flew the parachutes into each other - very carefully - and flew them attached like a four-masted schooner. At the same time, I was narrating the show from a wireless microphone. Having been an anchorman for so long, it's hard to keep quiet. Just remember the old adage, "You can always tell an old anchorman, you just can't tell him much!"

"Ladies and gentlemen, boys and girls, this is Arch Deal talking to you from under the highest parachute," I began, when suddenly something I didn't want to see came into view: the landing lights of a Boeing 737. It was at our altitude. I continued, "If you'll look just to the north, you'll see somebody else is trying to get into the act...a 737 jetliner!" Later, members of the audience confirmed they had not seen the jet until my description came through on the public address system. "This is going to be a close one!" I excitedly blurted, "If the jet hopefully misses, the jet wash (turbulence as the jet passes) is going to be lots of fun!" At about that time, the Canadian pilot saw the stacking parachutes and sharply veered to the west, passing about 500 feet from us, at the exact same altitude. I imagined one hundred or more Canadians looking out the window, exclaiming a collective, "EH!"

Amazingly, there was no jet wash and we continued to perform until we touched down for the appreciative crowd; a crowd that expected to see bodies falling to earth without benefit of parachutes.

My performers, Bill Brandon, Jamie Joanas and Gary Reich commented on the closeness of the 737. Reich said, "Did you see that 737? It passed 500 feet from us!" "Gary," I said, "that was after he saw us and had veered sharply out of the way." Only then did they realize the jetliner "had us," had not the pilot spotted the parachute canopies dead ahead. Apparently, approach control had cleared him to descent through our approved jump altitude. Oh well, just something to keep the adrenaline pumping.

On many occasions, someone has walked up to me and said, "I wouldn't do what you do for anything!" "Good," I would reply, "if everyone took up skydiving, no one would pay me." Also, I hear the question, "What if it happens again?" Or, as one lady wrote to me, "God will get you next time." For whatever reason, I believe He didn't want me at Cypress Gardens, but He did keep me on my toes.

Chapter 21
The Next Malfunction

Over Zephyrhills one fine spring day, our competition team, the Mile High Bunch, was busily falling through the sky, practicing to sharpen our free fall skills. At about 8,000 feet above the ground, somebody "railroaded" me; one of the sky divers, late in arriving in the formation, raced in too hot and slammed into me, and in particular, into my parachute backpack. The impact tore open my main container and dumped the parachute unceremoniously into the sky. It opened so abruptly and out of sequence, turning into a tangled mess.

This put me under a nasty parachute a mile and a half above ground. At least this meant I had some time to try to deal with the situation. So, for the next mile, I fumbled with the tangled mess, trying to get it to return to its original shape and fly me safely to the ground. It was a real struggle; particularly considering what happened the last time I tried to use my reserve parachute. What a "head trip" it was trying to unravel a hopeless situation and watching altitude unwind at the same time.

Some of my comrades had seen the pack knocked open and the spinning malfunction that resulted. Below, the spectators and the jumpers knew "somebody" had a problem. It appeared I would just about get the chute unwound when it would take off again, wrapping itself in a big ball. 3,500 feet...3,000 feet...2,500 feet...no more time to play, time to chop away this tangle of nylon and go for the reserve.

Talk about an adrenaline rush! My heart was pounding: 'Come on baby, you can do it, come on,' I prayed as I jettisoned the worthless snarl of fiber and lines. Now, I was in freefall again, accelerating toward the ground. I could be there in 15 seconds or less. I snatched at the ripcord of the reserve, pulling it with enough force to snatch a horse from a stall. I was pumped up! Then, that inexorable second of silence. 'Come on baby, open, open, open.' Suddenly, those prayers were answered as I threw my head back to watch the reserve canopy unfolding and snapping to life above me. Meanwhile, the main tangled mess that I had discarded was now flying through the sky as if someone had straightened out the mess. I thought, 'If that darn thing flares on landing, I'll burn it!' It didn't! Another jumper rushed to recover the chute as I prepared for an uneventful landing under the reserve canopy.

I'll never forget that reserve ride or the comment assistant drop zone operator Cy Fraser made, "Boy, Arch, that must have been some head trip!" Truer words were never spoken.

There would be more little problems, no doubt, but I would have to deal with them, having performed more than one thousand jumps for Miller Brewing Company into every major stadium in the country, from Seattle's Bumbershoot Festival to San Diego's Major Stadium; 12 times stopping off a half-dozen times in San Francisco for Fleet Week; a half dozen jumps into the Pasadena Rose Bowl; and thrice into the LA Coliseum. Across the nation, the jumps included every state except Alaska, Idaho, Utah and Vermont. We performed a full dozen times at Denver's Mile High Stadium; Portland's Civic Stadium, the Silver Bowl in Las Vegas, Boston's Nickerson Field and Miami's Orange Bowl. We stopped on the way to jump in New Hampshire, New York and the Carolinas.

Our experience in the Caribbean included the Bahamas, Grand Cayman Island and Aruba (one of the world's windiest islands).

Within 12 years and 1,000 shows, our team experienced seven malfunctions. Everyone landed safely on target. The last three came within two weeks of each other.

Fleet Week – San Francisco

Without a doubt, one of the most beautiful jump shows has been over San Francisco Bay, performing each year for the U.S. Navy Fleet Week. In my opinion, San Francisco is always a beautiful city but in October the weather is especially perfect. The temperatures are mild and winds are low, which is not the norm for the city by the bay. Our October, 1992 show was a real blast. We flew over the city in six beautiful Steerman Biplanes; one member of the Miller Six Pack in each vintage aircraft. At the signal from me, each of us climbed over the side of the open cockpit craft and fell into space. Starting at 6,500 feet, we were widely separated, but nevertheless headed toward one another to build our trademark Six Pack in the Sky.™ At the time, I was broadcasting live for KRQR-FM and KNBR-AM, two of the Bay Area's top radio stations. Simultaneously, the broadcasts were repeated over public address speakers for some half a million San Franciscans. What a joy, performing for over a million viewers and listeners while looking down at the beautiful downtown area and the famed Golden Gate Bridge.

All went well under jumper number six as he made his approach. Under me was Gary Reich of Zephyrhills; Charlie Moore of Plano, Texas; Bill Brandon of Zephyrhills; and Jeff Smith of Arlington, Texas; followed Bobby Coker of Dallas, Texas.

I must say, the Glide Path canopies we used for our demonstration jumps were the very best available in the world at that time. For performing into very tight, concrete areas or mile-high altitudes, they performed flawlessly. Nevertheless, no canopy can resist a wrap if you don't treat it right. Brandon started down the lines of Smith's canopy before his chute was fully "set." The result: canopy number five started to fold up and spiraled down and around hapless Smith on the bottom; an ugly word in canopy related work - a "wrap." They may start off slow but they only get uglier. And they get that way incredibly fast.

So, looking down, I'm telling one million San Franciscans, "We have a wrap, folks, two of our canopies have become entangled and they're spinning away through the sky." Within seconds, both Brandon and Smith had sized up their problems and were jettisoning their main chutes and going back into free fall, looking at San Francisco Bay again, accelerating to 120 miles per hour. Smoothly, as if in unison, both reserve canopies began to billow and take form.

"There you have it, ladies and gentlemen, boys and girls; both of our jumpers have left their tangled main chutes and deployed their reserves, just as they're trained to do." I tried to act very blasé about the whole thing. Like it was just a part of the act, but it wasn't. You could die in situations like that if you don't act with coolness and precision. "Both men," I said with extreme hope, "will land on the intended target at Aquatic Park." Within half a minute, both performers were flaring their canopies for perfect touchdowns in that tiny parcel of grass at the foot of the trolley turntable. What a show! CNN repeated the performance several times the next (Sunday) morning. It was exciting and it was perfectly safe. The news media was particularly favorable in its reporting. It stated that there was a major problem but the professional performers took correct and immediate action and all landed safely! It was, after all, a highly favorable report.

There was one substantial change. Brandon, who usually sipped a non-alcoholic Miller Sharps after each jump, guzzled a couple of Miller Genuine Drafts at the handy TGI Friday's.

Talk about luck, I broadcast on the way down, if anyone found the chutes they could be returned for a reward. Within minutes, a couple from Novato, California, Matt and Lynn Munson, walked up carrying two piles of white nylon: our jettisoned chutes. It was greatly appreciated, and they were rewarded! It was the first time the Fleet Week had received national television coverage.

Two weeks later we found ourselves warming under the Caribbean sun of the Cayman Islands where we were to perform for Pirate's Week, one of the Island's most tourist-drawing events.

Saturday morning prior to the show we sat enjoying breakfast and talking over the game plan for the skydiving gig. As luck would have it, I mentioned I hadn't had a malfunction within the past 12 years! Somehow, I knew I shouldn't have said that.

On the way from Georgetown to the Cayman Airport I wondered, 'should I repack this rig? I have no idea who jumped it last or who packed it. Should I? Nah, it'll be just fine!' As we climbed over the beautiful jewel of the Caribbean a few cumulous clouds began to move over the town, forcing us to abandon our plans to build the six pack and substitute, instead, our low show.

The winds at this time were just under 16 knots, our maximum legal wind speed. I lined up the Cessna 206 jump plane by giving a few small corrections to pilot Tom Giton and prepared to exit. "Good luck and have a great jump," I shouted to the rest of the crew as I flung my body into space.

Within seconds, I reached for the handle of the pilot chute and flung it into the 120 mile per hour wind blast. The reaction was not good. Immediately, the chute began to spin and spin, harder and harder. Looking at the mess, it was obvious this darn thing is never going to work! Wow, I'm getting awfully low too. Immediately, I grabbed at the Velcro handle to release the main chute and in a half-second yanked the reserve ripcord handle. In a flash, the gorgeous blue Glide Path Maverick reserve was open and flying.

I looked in the direction of the drop zone, 'No way.' I thought. I would never make it. I'm too darn low to clear the building and power lines. Below, however, was one of the most beautiful patches of green you've ever seen. In seconds, I hooked a low turn in and landed in the cool grass.

Within a minute or so, a native of the Caymans found his way to me and offered a ride to the intended target. What a gentleman! Arriving at the target, the dockside in George Town, I learned that Karen and my daughter, Michelle, had never seen the opening of the chute. A tall building beside the target cut off their vision as I spiraled out of sight. From that vantage point, it must have appeared that I "went in" again, a prospect no one would want to face and certainly something l wouldn't care to display.

There was a humorous side to the malfunction. At the time of the jump, I was being interviewed live on Z-99 Radio in the Caymans. As I fought with the spinning chute, a young lady started the interview. "Well, Arch, I see you've opened your parachute. How does it look from up there?" "It looks pretty ugly right now!" I yelled back, "I have an ugly malfunction of this parachute and I have to get rid of it right away!" "Well," she continued, "it looks great from here, we're looking forward to your landing." "Me too," I thought, as I jettisoned the unmanageable paraphernalia and opened a beautiful chute that worked! My team mates, Derek Thomas (a Brit, who manufactured the Sunpath Javelin parachute container I use for my team), the late Gary Reich of Zephyrhills and Jamie Joanas, watched the display from the airplane, came around for another pass and landed smiling on the target. Would you believe, we recovered that jumble of nylon I had tossed away? It landed on a Caymanians roof and waited for our pickup the next morning.

The following year, I continued to get my knees in the breeze as often as possible and amassed over six thousand jumps. Sounds like a huge number but I know jumpers who were over 15 to 25 thousand jumps. It obviously becomes habit forming.

Occasionally, I'm approached by a well-wisher who finally asks "You're not still jumping are you?" "Of course," I reply, "what else could go wrong?" "You need to see a psychiatrist." I'm told. "I do," is my stock reply, "he jumps with me." This is another truism. For over 25 years, a great skydiving friend has been Dr. Stephen Groff, a noted psychiatrist in the Tampa area. I've used that line for over 25 years and, only recently, revealed to Dr. Groff how I had involved him. Groff, who is a great skydiver and pilot replied, "Now, if I could go find a psychiatrist to jump with me!" Asked why he skydives, the answer is almost always the same with every jumper, "Because I enjoy it!" You could no more describe the sensation to a non-jumper than you would be able to describe the difference between the taste of an apple or orange…or a color to a person who has always been blind. Groff, incidentally, has thousands of jumps and is an instructor pilot - flies his own helicopter. He formerly had an apartment in New Jersey, across the East

River, with an unobstructed view of the Twin Towers. He said he and Ina used to enjoy the fabulous view, however, after 9/11, he was so saddened by the terrible loss of life and the tower; he did not renew his lease. Instead he returned to Tampa. Educated in Amsterdam, Groff also took up skydiving there and back in the 60s became a world champion under the chute.

From life as an active news reporter, I established a business called The Voice of Business and opened a studio to record narrations and messages on hold. The business covered industries from the east to the west coast. Later, I added another dimension to my life, trading all of the 50 some years of broadcasting/television reporting for teaching students of broadcasting at Hillsborough Community College in Tampa's Ybor City section. Teaching, I found, is truly a rewarding experience, one most young people can't appreciate. However, the light in the eyes of a student is more than enough reward. In fact, my first class asked to take me to dinner. "First," I said, "you'll be graded before the dinner and I also have to check with the dean's office to make sure there is no impropriety in accepting the dinner." The dean's office said it was a first, but totally acceptable. Gives you a warm fuzzy feeling!

Chapter 22
Gosh, It Happened Again!

In August of 2002, the lure of the sky brought me once again to Zephyrhills and the "call of the sky." It was during the "Dog Days of Summer"…hot and hotter, with matching humidity. But then, that wasn't unusual in Florida. Did I mention, I live in Florida under one condition… air conditioning? At least it's cool when you climb to altitude. The normal lapse rate of temperature is: it cools down 3.5 degrees every thousand feet you climb. Therefore, a hot and sultry 90 degrees on the ground would be about 43 degrees at

Free falling and feeling free over Zephyrhills, Florida

13,500 feet… and then, there is the "chill factor," the cooling effect of the wind, through which you are diving over 120 miles per hour. I understand the chill factor only works to about 50 miles per hour but you get the drift. It's refreshing, but only for a short while. When you get down to a couple thousand feet, the heat and humidity returns.

It just so happened that a young lady of 50 wanted to celebrate her 50th birthday by forming (in the sky) a big 5 - 0! Sounds like a great idea. Why not? Several months earlier, we helped a gentleman (Late Jake) celebrate his 80th by forming a giant 8 - 0 in the sky. It was a blast. Mucho cerveza fria were served that evening. It went off without a hitch. One of my most common jokes about skydiving, when someone asks me, "Are you still skydiving... after what happened to you?" "Sure," I always replied, "What else could go wrong!"

It took the Tampa Bay Buccaneers 27 years to finally capture a Super Bowl title! And it was 27 years since the nearly fatal impact at Cypress Gardens.

We gathered a great gaggle of skydivers and went about figuring the formation for this lady's 50th birthday celebration. It was a beautiful skydiving day as we happily geared up and marched to the twin Otter jump plane! This is a marvelous jump aircraft, capable of carrying 21 skydivers to 13,500 feet in less than 10 minutes.

In that short length of time, we were in position over Zephyhills, Florida and the Sky Dive City Drop Zone. Nothing unusual about this, as I had done this six thousand times before. No bragging here! Many of my colleagues have over ten thousand jumps!

Over the exit point, we began to put the "floaters" out first. Floaters climb out and hang before the opening in the fuselage and others climb forward. With a "ready...set...go," we all dove out of the aircraft in just over a second and began to build the formation for the birthday lady! This was good; with pride, we easily put together the formation, with each diver saluting one another and especially the birthday lady.

In spite of how many people may regard skydiving, it is not a reckless sport entered into with wild abandon. Discipline is one of the most important parts of a good skydive. Otherwise, you may wind up as a statistic... and part of the landscape!

We plan ahead and this size formation would separate at about 4,500 feet, giving each skydiver a chance to turn 180 degrees and track (or glide) away from the tight formation. The center diver will usually open his chute immediately and is pulled out of the formation. Gliding away, the remaining jumpers stack their opening every 500 feet with the lowest opening at 2,000 feet above ground level. That's the altitude opening minimum level for expert rated skydivers.Climbing out of the aircraft to hang by the open door, I waited for the command, "Ready, set, go." I left, as always on "set," command to fly out of the way and enter the 5 - 0 formation. So far, so good (said the guy disarming a bomb). At four thousand feet, it was break-off time. Everyone turns 180 degrees and tracks away from the center. It, in effect, gives us "opening separation" much like the skiers leaving the ramp to glide their bodies as far as possible before making a smooth landing.

At two thousand feet above the Zephyrhills landscape I cleared the sky, waved off and deployed my parachute. Wouldn't you know if I would wind up in a snivel? A snivel is where the parachute for whatever reason decides to be slow on opening. It has happened a few times before but always opened. This time, however, the snivel was much longer and I was obviously getting closer to terra firma. Gaining my separation, I looked right and left, above and below and observed I was clear of the other free-fallers… then I pulled.

Instead of a smooth sudden opening, I found my main chute was sniveling, being very slow to inflate. 'Come on,' I thought to myself, 'open, baby, open!' But the recalcitrant chute was still not opening! Time to go, can't wait for "ground-rush," gotta get away from the main chute and air out my reserve.

'Gotta cut-away,' I thought, and went for the release system that freed me from the recalcitrant main parachute. Then I snatched the ripcord to open my reserve chute. Already very low, due to my own inaction, the chute didn't have full time to inflate for me to release the brakes and turn into the wind for a landing.

Obviously I was low and not in a very favorable spot. With a sudden turn, it was "lights out."

I smacked in…very HARD… in fact, so hard I broke both femurs between the knee and hip. The right one was a compound fracture. Not very pretty, but I didn't get a chance to look at it. The impact slammed me into the ground. And, in spite of a full-coverage helmet, it was night-night time! Later, in the hospital, I found I had a sizeable bruise on my right temple. Thank God for that helmet.

I awoke in Tampa General Hospital with titanium rods inserted into each femur. Let me tell you, that really slows down your dancing. I always kid, and tell people not to go into a hospital…it's full of sick people…you can catch something in there. Needless to say, there I was, and there I would stay for 21 miserable days! Ever try hospital food? Near the end of my stay, I had to prove I could travel around a full sized basketball court four times in a walker…and then prove my prowess on a Stairmaster before I could win release.

During my recovery, I was an adjunct professor at Hillsborough Community College teaching the easy stuff for me: television and radio. This I truly enjoyed as I trekked in each day on my walker to lecture the students. I loved teaching and I had great students. I guess it's unlike middle school and high school! These students were there to learn and work with equipment I never had when I tried to get into the same field. This was a great opportunity and one I will always cherish.

About the same time, I began to do narrations for the Hillsborough County TV station and work at my own business, the Voice of Business. This was the business I started years ago, utilizing my voice for narrations and messages on hold. This included a few national accounts like Ranger American Security and Home Team Services, along with using my past All-Star contacts to produce messages on hold for many Miller Beer Distributors nationally. Amazingly, I even performed for the Leeds Theatre in England (seems they had many English voices and wanted a state-side voice).

It seemed the Cayman Islands was to celebrate the 50th anniversary of commercial aviation on the island. Since I made the first ever parachute jump, they felt I was a tiny part of that history. In short, they wanted a jump! Well, I told them I couldn't quiet jump at that stage but would bring a top-flight crew of jumpers to the island and I would narrate the jumps. That worked out very well. And we all had a great time.

To this day, I will always have a very warm place in my heart for the Cayman Islands and the great Caymanians. When (with lots of luck) I hit the lottery, I'll buy a home there for the cooler days in Florida!

It would be hard to imagine what some have called a "normal" life. To me, the challenge is always there. The challenge of news reporting, of always trying to "get it first, but first ... get it right!"

Arch with World Champion Dancer Denise Rivera

After smacking into the ground too often (some of it my own fault)...and after 13 major bone fractures, I still love to skydive and to fly. Further, I train now for ballroom dancing with a lovely former world champion, Denise Rivera.

Page 116

The freedom of flight I feel has always been the dream of mankind; whether in an aircraft or on the wings of man, the ability of mankind to fly, if only for a minute, has been the desire of many.

One a cold and cloudy day in Great Britain, September, 1941, Gillespie wrote to his parents, about High Flight!. He scribbled it on the back of an envelope and wrote lasting words about flight!

Oh! I have slipped the surly bonds of Earth

And danced the skies on laughter-silvered wings;

Sunward I've climbed, and joined the tumbling mirth

Of sun-split clouds, — and done a hundred things

You have not dreamed of — wheeled and soared and swung

High in the sunlit silence. Hov'ring there,

I've chased the shouting wind along, and flung

My eager craft through footless halls of air. . . .

Up, up the long, delirious burning blue

I've topped the wind-swept heights with easy grace

Where never lark, or ever eagle flew —

And, while with silent, lifting mind I've trod

The high untrespassed sanctity of space,

Put out my hand, and touched the face of God.

— John Gillespie Magee, Jr

His Spitfire collided with an Oxford Trainer high over Roxham, England in the county of Devonshire at an altitude of 400 feet. As it plunged toward earth, a farmer saw Gillespie push back the canopy and stand to jump... but he was too low.

While he was lost, his words became immortal for all those who venture into the sky... whether a pilot, astronaut or skydiver.

Chapter 23
9/11/2001

As a former Miller Lite All-Star, I was fortunate to be included in the promotion that Miller and NCL Cruise line concocted: The Miller Lite All-Star Cruises!

What an opportunity. We were chosen to take a free seven-day cruise with all expenses paid, including a wife or friend. It included first class airfare, all taxis and other transportation…the full cruise with all excursions included… and an unlimited bar tab! After the first few cruises, I limited my intake of alcohol… but the cruises truly "ruined me." I was chosen to take at least two cruises each year! I assumed they either liked the way I did it or would keep sending me to learn how! After ten years with Miller (they now belong to South African Brewery), I started paying for my own. I regard it as the very best way to travel.

On one of the cruises I invited my former father-in-law, Geoffrey Townsley, along. Later, he insisted on inviting me to take a Mediterranean Cruise and I did. Flying from London, we boarded the ship in the Mediterranean for the seven-day vacation. As fate would have it, we arrived at our first port, the port of Beirut, Lebanon, on the morning of September 11, 2001… 911!

There is a seven hour difference between Beirut and New York City! We boarded a taxi and had a great tour of the city, pock-marked by bullets and missiles. I found the city was largely westernized, especially for the young ladies I observed in the shopping centers. The taxi driver tried to delay our return to the cruise ship with the intention of earning extra money for side trips. However, we knew the ship would certainly sail without us if we didn't return… so return we did.

Boarding the ship I learned that an aircraft had crashed into one of the Twin Towers in New York. I grabbed a cup of coffee and sat down to watch. Then I saw the second plane collide. Then, this old newsman knew we were under attack.

Chat with John F. Kennedy

The last time I felt this way was in 1963, four days after spending a pleasant chat with Jack Kennedy, four days before his assassination. I, along with every caring American was stunned!

There is always at least one event that stands out in the career of any newsman who worked in Tampa news media in November of 1963. It was the day-long visit of America's youthful 35th President of the United States, John F. Kennedy.

Up to that point The Gasparilla Pirate Invasion and Parade had been the biggest news gathering project for us. But Gasparilla happened every year and was very predictable. A visit like this from John F. Kennedy was once in a lifetime, as we later found out. Even though reporters had his schedule we really didn't know exactly what to expect.

Everybody looked forward to Kennedy's trip here. It was the first time an American president had ever come to Tampa to spend nearly an entire day and with so many different appearances scheduled.

President Kennedy's afternoon in Tampa would be much different from the campaign stop he made here in October of 1960. I was assigned as a WFLA reporter to cover Kennedy's speech on the west (Pierce Street) side of the old Hillsborough County Courthouse, which at that time housed most county government offices. I was pretty neutral about his visit then although lots of others influenced by the national media were beginning to be enamored with the youthful energy of the rising political star. There was a sizeable crowd of people there and we covered his stop live.

By the fall of 1963, we in the news business knew Kennedy had some political vulnerability in Florida and the 1964 presidential campaign was closing in. I think Kennedy and his political advisors sensed there were many voters who were smitten by the JFK persona but were not keen on him politically and felt he had made some serious blunders, particularly in his failure to back CIA-trained invaders from the United States during the 1961 Bay of Pigs invasion designed to liberate Cuba from the rule of Fidel Castro. His trip to Tampa and Miami early that week was designed to strengthen some political alliances, somewhat the same purpose as was his trip to Dallas at the end of that week.

Kennedy's November 18, 1963 visit did not require us to spend a great deal of time with logistical planning…just making sure that close to a dozen staffers were planted in the right places, got their film shot, and returned to the station in time to ease production of the evening news. We gathered in reporters and stringers from every bureau to help in the effort that day.

However, getting ready for the evening news coverage of the President's activities would be somewhat more complex than we were used to and required extraordinary coordination. We were not only preparing coverage of the visit for the 6 o'clock report but we were producing a half hour special on his visit to be broadcast at 7:30 that evening.

My reportorial responsibility in the field that day was to cover President Kennedy's arrival at MacDill Air Force Base. I arrived at the Officer's Club about 15 minutes before him, just before noon. At that time, there was hardly anybody outside waiting for him. He was driven up to the front curb, got out of his limo, and said to me, "Hi, nice day." At first, I was in awe of being in the presence of this legendary President but he quickly put me at ease. It was an extremely casual encounter where he got away from everybody for a while. I was the only newsman there, had my camera with me, but he totally disarmed me with his comments and during the few minutes of talking to him I sort of forgot why I was there. It's very rare to be able to speak personally to a man like John Kennedy and we continued our brief talk before his handlers moved him on. I found he was just a great guy who had a much better job that I did.

I was in the right place at the right time, basically. I didn't wait for him to come out of the Officer's Club. Since I had my chat and got my film, I headed directly back to WFLA, where we started coordinating all our other field people to put the 6 o'clock news show together… that night a bit more complicated to do than usual.

Kennedy's assassination four days later was devastating. I was at home getting ready for work when I got a call from the station that he had been shot. I was paralyzed by the news, it really threw me. You're never ready for something like that. Suddenly there was an urgency to get to the station so I threw myself together and took off.

There was an incredible air of sadness that sort of settled on the city, like a fog that had moved in rapidly. The general mood of everyone shifted quickly as the news of the President being shot and the later announcement of his death moved through the populace with the speed of lightening. Within an hour, Tampa went from a vibrant business center to a city that was shut down and in mourning. I've never experienced that again, even to this day. I always imagined that our experience that day may have been similar to that of Britons when they heard of the passing of Princess Diana in 1997.

We prepared the entire local show for the evening of November 22, 1963... but it never aired. In its place was NBC's continuous coverage of the assassination, which, to me at the time, was pretty pathetic and slow moving in gathering facts. But the pace picked up once things shifted from Dallas to Washington.

I'd have to say the coverage of all three networks, even the distant third and poorly staffed ABC, rose to new heights during that time. All of us who worked that weekend matured in ways we would never have otherwise imagined. It was the first time for many of us to be such a part of history, covering the assassination of a President who had just walked and talked in our city four days before.

Back to the Mediterranean and 9-11

After that horrendous attack on the Twin Towers, everything changed. It was the first terrorist attack on American soil. This also drastically changed the course of the cruise we were on, after only one day.

It was planned as a vacation cruise to the Mediterranean, a chance to finally see the Pyramids and the Sphinx. The first day we made at stop in Beirut. I was travelling with my former father-in-law, now a friend, a tried and true Brit by the name of Geoffrey Townsley. Even though the city was pock-marked by bullets and shell fire, I enjoyed the city, which was very modern on the outskirts. The taxi driver tried to persuade us to stay longer and travel further. Our ship, however, would have sailed without us...and that would not have been a pleasant night. Arriving back on board I learned a plane had accidentally flown into one of the Twin Towers. I grabbed a cup of java and set back to see another behemoth jet slam into the other tower. This, I knew was a terrorist attack (and I would say, "Damn political correctness, this is a terrorist attack!") Everyone was stunned. Shortly afterwards we learned we could not enter the port in Egypt but elected to sail to Greek and Turkish ports.

Two days later, as I strolled on the deck, a young cruise staff member stopped me to ask, "You're Arch Deal, aren't you?"

"Well, yes," I replied, "but with a thousand passengers on this ship, how did you know?" "Because," she added, "you are the only American on this ship!" Now, that get's your attention! However, there were no problems! Most of the passengers were Brits or Scandinavians, including an interesting

Scotsman who wore his kilts proudly and always watched carefully as the ladies walked by! No problem there, I did the same! As we chatted on deck, a pretty young lady walked by! I commented, "A thing of beauty is a job forever!" By jove, the Scotsman countered, "May I use that line?" "Certainly, that's okay by me but I think it came from the poet Keats..." (trying to recall my college days!) "Anyway," said the Scot, "I will use that!"

photo by Tony Hathaway

In the following days in a Turkish port I strolled down a street among the many vendors and tried to enjoy the sights. At the same time, I noticed two Turkish teenagers watching me. I ignored the stares when suddenly they rushed up to me asking, "Are you an American?" "Yes," I proudly proclaimed. With that, both of the boys gave me warm hugs...truly a note of friendship and understanding!

Coming home was a truly different experience. As a newsman, I had been able to walk into any airport terminal. Now, that has changed, perhaps forever!

When I finally arrived back in Florida, I gathered up my largest American Flag and headed for Zephyrhills. I got ace skydiver-cameraman Tony

Hathaway to jump with me, following behind to film the sight of 'Ole Glory' unfurled and flying over the land of the free. The picture received national recognition in many magazines and newspapers.

Interestingly, many people say, "I don't see your face in the picture!" I always reply, "I'm not important! Our Flag is!"

Speaking of skydivers, one of the most prominent is former president George Herbert Walker Bush. He receives outstanding accolades from me and it has nothing to do with politics!

During World War II, Bush piloted one of four Grumman TBM Avenger aircraft that attacked the Japanese installations on Chichi Jima Island. During their attack, the Avengers encountered intense anti-aircraft fire; Bush's aircraft was hit by flak and his engine caught on fire. Despite his plane being on fire, Bush completed his attack and released bombs over his target, scoring several damaging hits. With his engine afire, Bush flew several miles from the island where he bailed out of the aircraft. Since that necessary jump, Bush (with nothing to prove) has made four sport parachute jumps! He added after one of them, "I'm not telling anyone to skydive, I'm just saying: Do something! Keep Active!"

Often I am asked why I continue to skydive. As long as I am not a danger to myself or anyone else, I will continue!

Jump again? A musician cannot give up his music or the artist his paint brush; being a pilot and skydiver has become a very important part of my life. To feel the air as you dive out of an airplane and swoop down to join your fellow skydivers and perform graceful patterns in the sky is beyond comprehension…unless you've been there. You never say, "Never."

For whatever reason, I was spared after falling three thousand feet. For that, I am eternally grateful to God. I often kid when people ask me how I survived such a fall. I irreverently reply, "God wasn't ready for me… and the devil was afraid I would take over. That's only a joke folks!"

Being a television news reporter, pilot and skydiver, and a proud father of 5, have been the most thrilling parts of my life. My kids have been and will always be the most important accomplishment in life. They, of course, are all different…but all loved equally. They somehow accept Dad's skydiving quirks!

I would never try to talk anyone into the sport...but it has become a part of me! Like President George W. Bush, who made his first jump when his TBM plane was shot down over the pacific during WW II, the parachute saved his life...and he later made at least five sport jumps. I understand this can become a part of your life... as it has for me!

Chapter 24
A Tragic Loss

To this point, this has been a very happy and a very lucky story. However, life isn't always happy-go-lucky. I found this with the death of my daughter: my first born! She was first, born 57 years ago. I always had love for all of my children…four young ladies and my son. It is truly an American tragedy. As a TV News anchor, I have always felt comfortable speaking before millions.

However, the most difficult speech I have ever made (and I pray none of you ever have to regardless of the child's age) was at the service of my child. Nothing could ever have been so challenging and hurtful. But, Karen would have said, "Dad, you can do it, I know you can!" She would have expected this of me! With her love and encouragement, I somehow made it through…pausing occasionally to try to compose myself. Dear God, how that hurt! And all of my children: Diane, Doug, Shari and Michelle were there… and, yes, so were my three former wives. Each welcomed me with a sincere hug!

Weeks later, a special Memorial Concert for Karen was held at Skipper's Smokehouse in North Tampa, where Karen had played just a month earlier. She was happiest at her keyboards; playing the music she (and I) loved so much. A tribute performance was scheduled to continue to honor this bright, shining star of music. Her music brought her the love of thousands. She knew that thousands loved her. Even the legendary rock and soul singer Little Richard said a prayer for her at his Hollywood home.

I joke when I say, "Falling three thousand feet really doesn't hurt; it's only the sudden stop that hurts." However, losing a child is something no one should ever have to endure. I know I was truly blessed to have five loving children. I hold them close and never forget to tell them that I love them. We may not always love what our children do but we love them regardless! Make sure they always know your love!

To try to cope with this terrible loss, I will always cherish the memories of Karen and all of my children. I will continue to skydive…at the young age of 79! Perhaps it now will be a bit of an escape for me. I think Karen would have expected me to! She always observed, "We all have to get older…but we don't have to get old!'

I jumped into the San Diego Stadium twelve times.

First for the Padres, then for the Chargers, San Diego State and a Motor Cross. At one of those games, after I landed at the center of the field, my daughter, Karen, ran out to greet me.

This picture with daughter Karen at San Diego stadium is one of my most cherished pictures!